Lightning Literature & Composition
Eighth Grade: Teacher Guide
Second Edition

**Preparing for High School Composition Skills
by Responding to Great Literature**

The difference between the right word and the almost-right word
is the difference between the lightning and the lightning bug.
—Mark Twain

Elizabeth Kamath

For Toby and Simon

Edited by Hewitt Staff

Mailing address . . . . . P. O. Box 9, Washougal WA 98671-0009
Phone . . . . (360) 835-8708; (800) 348-1750
E-mail . . . . info@hewitthomeschooling.com
Website . . . . www.hewitthomeschooling.com

Published July 2006. Second Edition June 2011
Printed in the United States of America
21 20 19 18 17 16 15   7 6 5 4 3 2

ISBN 10: 1-57896-237-4
ISBN 13: 978-1-57896-237-2

Table of Contents

week 16-20 of IEW, Y1 LB

REQUIRED BOOKS FOR THIS COURSE

You need unabridged copies of the following books:

Stories & Poems for Extremely Intelligent Children by Harold Bloom
Treasure Island by Robert L. Stevenson
A Day of Pleasure by Isaac B. Singer
A Christmas Carol by Charles Dickens
The Hobbit by J. R. R. Tolkien
My Family and Other Animals by Gerald Durrell
To Kill a Mockingbird by Harper Lee

How to Use Lightning Literature & Composition for Grade 8

This Teacher Guide is meant to help you help your student through the Lightening Literature Student Guide and Workbook for Grade 8.

After this introduction, which includes a weekly planning schedule, the teaching helps in this guide follow the course in the order the stories are read. In other words, you'll find all the Teacher Guide help for "A Crazy Tale" first, then everything for *Treasure Island*, etc., rather than all the answers to the comprehension questions in one place.

The following is an overview of the different sections of the Student Guide, the Workbook, Discussion Questions (found only in this teacher's guide), and what this Teacher Guide addresses for each section.

Student Guide

WELCOME TO LIGHTNING LITERATURE

This tells the student how to use the Student Guide and Workbook and what I hope they'll get out of the course. There is no additional information in this Teacher Guide for this section.

INTRODUCTIONS/WHILE YOU READ

Each introduction gives a brief biography of the author or authors used in the lesson. The student is told what the literary lesson will be about and given some questions to consider while reading the selection(s). There is no additional information in this Teacher Guide for these sections.

VOCABULARY LISTS

These lists are not meant to substitute for separate vocabulary work. I strongly recommend you use some sort of vocabulary program along with this series; I particularly like *Vocabulary From Classical Roots,* but whatever vocabulary program you like will be fine. These lists are simply an easy reference for students if they encounter words in the reading that they do not know. (Obviously, students have different vocabulary sets, so your students may encounter words they don't know that aren't listed here. As with any reading, they should either divine the word from the context or look it up in a dictionary.) These lists do not include every meaning of the words, only the meaning used in the book; nor do they include pronunciation.

If you wish, look over each vocabulary list, choose words you would most like your student to learn, and create your own vocabulary lessons from these.

COMPREHENSION QUESTIONS

The comprehension questions help you discern the student's attention to and understanding of the reading material. How you approach these questions depends on your student's current level of reading comprehension. For students who are strong in reading comprehension, I suggest waiting until Friday, or whenever a reading selection has been completed, to have them complete all the comprehension questions covering that week's reading. If a few weeks of this result in consistent scores of 95 percent or higher, you might try stretching this to longer periods of time—first a week and a half, then two weeks. Feel free to stop when the student's scores are hovering around the low 90s, especially if your student is very grade-conscious. The point is not to frustrate the student, but to challenge.

On the other hand, if your student has historically had difficulty with comprehension, then test at every chapter (if the questions are set up that way) or at the end of each day. Leave time so that if the student misses a question you can review the reading together to see the correct answer in context. Once your student scores 100 percent on five tests in a row using this method, only give the comprehension questions every other day (either Tuesday, Thursday, and Friday or Monday, Wednesday, and Friday—don't try to test after a weekend). Again, review material that is missed, and when five tests in a row are perfect, test once on Wednesday and once on Friday. Continue this successive increase in time until testing is only once a week, then follow the directions in the paragraph above.

You may find that your student tests better on these questions for some books than others. For example, test scores may go down if your student really enjoys *Treasure Island*, but does not find *The Hobbit* as engaging. This is neither surprising nor reason for concern. I do recommend that any tests below 75 percent be reviewed. (You may choose to set the bar even higher.)

This Teacher Guide contains the answers to the Comprehension Questions.

LITERARY LESSONS

These are really the heart and soul of the Lightning Literature series (along with the writing exercises). Here, students learn about such things as setting, figurative language, and character. The lessons are written to the students. They cite passages from the literature the student has just read and sometimes give additional examples. This Teacher Guide gives suggestions for more practice with the concepts in the lessons; if your student easily masters the lesson, you may not need to use these.

Mini-Lessons

In addition to the main lesson there is one boxed mini-lessons per chapter. These sometimes relate to the reading and sometimes introduce other composition skills. This Teacher Guide gives suggestions for more practice with the concepts in the lessons; if your student easily masters the lesson, you may not need to use these.

Many of the mini-lessons in the Grade 8 Guide concern writing a research report. This is an important skill to learn for high school and college. The writing exercises often include research paper opportunities, and I suggest students choose at least one research paper this year. I also urge you to assign research papers in other classes as well, such as history, science, art, and music. Feel free to let students choose the topics for these papers, as long as the topics coincide with what is being studied. (For example, if you're studying American history this year, it would make little sense for the student to write a paper on the beginning of the Roman Empire.) The student should apply the skills being learned in this class regarding composition to those papers as well. Too often I see high-school students write proper research papers for English, but substandard research papers with no citations and no bibliographies for other classes. It is important for students to get into the habit of applying their composition skills to all their work in all classes.

Writing Exercises

The writing exercises at the end of each chapter should be done after the workbook exercises are complete. Students who have the time can complete a second writing exercise (this is scheduled for in the lesson plans). I strongly recommend that students complete at least one paper per chapter though. Many of the exercises relate to the literary lessons, but not all. For example, some are research papers or opinion essays. I encourage students to choose exercises based on their interests, but it's also important to pick a variety of exercises. Frequently, for example, students who are very good at creative writing choose only creative exercises, and thus could go an entire year without writing a research paper or literary analysis. I would recommend students of this type choose at least two research options and two analyses, allowing the rest of their papers to be creative.

When correcting your student's writing, strive to be as positive as possible, while still pointing out problems. It can be easy to fall into the trap of simply noting the mistakes, but students learn as much from finding out what they did well as what they did poorly. Whether to have a student rewrite a paper is an individual decision. Certainly, any paper that is simply unacceptable for whatever reason (large number of mistakes with grammar and mechanics, inappropriate content, etc.) should be rewritten. Smaller problems can also benefit from rewriting, but if your student does not like writing or is easily discouraged, this may be too much. Use your judgment, but err on the side of keeping your student happy and interested in writing.

This Teacher Guide tells you which assignments are easier and which are more difficult and why. Depending on your student's writing experience and skill, you may want to direct them to certain exercises for appropriate challenge without overwhelming them.

Workbook

Students should complete the workbook pages after they are done with the reading and lesson but before they try any of the writing exercises. There are seven types of workbook pages: **[L]** exercises relating to the major *literary lessons,* **[M]** exercises relating to the *mini-lessons,* **[T]** *thinking skill* pages, **[G]** exercises that review *grammar and mechanics,* **[A]** exercises that help students practice literary analysis, **[P]** *puzzles,* and **[E]** *extra-challenge* pages. Students should always complete any of the first five types (each chapter does not necessarily have all five of these). The last two are optional.

workbook pages relating to the literary lessons [L], and mini-lessons [M], and Analysis [A] should always be completed, whether the student has easily understood the concepts of the lesson or struggled (though you may wish to do some review first if your student has struggled). The pages are meant to reinforce the lessons and give practice in these skills before attempting the writing exercises.

workbook pages relating to thinking skills [T] should be completed by all students, even if the skill being tested is not something that you have covered before. These are skills students should at least begin acquiring in the junior high-school years. Glance ahead at these pages, and feel free to give some guidance if necessary.

workbook pages relating to grammar [G] are meant to be review. I have chosen grammar skills which have usually been taught before 8th grade or early in the 8th-grade year. Not everyone follows the same scope and sequence though, so look ahead at these pages as well. If you see that your student is about to encounter a grammar page on a concept they have not yet covered, postpone that page until they have covered the concept (or you might be able to use the page to teach the concept).

Puzzles [P] and extra challenge pages [E] are optional. There are one crossword puzzle and one word search puzzle per lesson covering aspects of the reading and the lessons learned. The extra challenge pages cover a variety of language arts topics, but these are not topics that have been taught in this class yet. Look ahead to these; if you have covered the topic then have your student complete the workbook page. If you have not, you may skip it, or you can use the page as a teaching tool.

I did not intend any of these workbook exercises as tests. How heavily you wish to emphasize grading them is up to you. The answer keys do provide the number of possible points for most workbook exercises, but you can also ignore this and simply go over any wrong answers with your student. I did not include possible points for more subjective pages (like rewriting something in the student's own words). You may still issue grades for these pages as well, if you wish, but you will have to develop your own system.

This Teacher Guide contains the answers to the workbook pages.

Discussion Questions

These are included in this Teacher Guide rather than the Student Guide. They are not required, but you may like to bring them up with your student. They are meant to bring the student beyond just the literary aspects of the work to questions that deal with their lives. These questions should not be done in a testing or other formal manner; rather, think of them more as dinner-table conversation. If you have read the material yourself, you can come up with your own questions. But if you haven't the time to do this, these questions can help get a discussion started.

Why Use Lightning Literature & Composition for Grade 8

The Importance of Reading

Here are some reasons to read great literature, in no particular order:
- To develop an appreciation for, and understanding of, literature
- To expose oneself to great writing, thus enhancing one's own writing
- To learn about other times and cultures
- To expand and refine one's view of the world
- To increase one's understanding of human nature—both its triumphant and tragic sides
- To learn lessons in honesty, integrity, courage, and a myriad of other moral and ethical values
- To form concrete images in one's mind of how these abstract values are expressed in and between people
- To revel in the beauty, elegance, and surprises that only great writers can regularly coax from language
- For pleasure

Any one of these reasons can be sufficient for reading, but the last certainly helps all the others. I have tried to choose literature appropriate for 8th-grade students that would address at least one (and usually several) of these points. Of course, your student will enjoy some of these works more than others, but I also tried to choose books, short stories, and poems that are pleasurable to read.

If you still read aloud to your junior high student, I encourage you to continue for as long as you both enjoy it. There is no age when one is too old to be read to. Talk about the story or poem as you go along, choosing natural breaking points to do so if it is a long story.

Whether or not you still read to your child, it's very likely that your child is now reading on their own as well. To get the most out of their reading, I recommend they do the following:

- Have a comfortable, well-lit spot, free from interruptions
- Try to read in blocks of at least half an hour
- Keep a reading journal of their thoughts on their reading
- Discuss their reading with you, other family members, and/or friends

READING POETRY

Reading poetry can pose special problems, especially if your student hasn't read much poetry before. Poetry often has unusual syntax, and doesn't usually have the context that prose does to aid with unfamiliar words. Poetry also contains a lot of figurative and symbolic language, and the student may not have much familiarity with this.

One exercise that can help a student understand a poem is to write a prose version of it. This will not always be necessary, but if a student is really struggling to understand a poem, it can help to transform the unfamiliar poetic syntax into the more familiar paragraphs.

The Importance of Writing

Writing is important for so many reasons. Very few people become professional writers, but every day people write essays for college, reports for work, or letters to family, newspapers, or politicians. Learning to write clearly, powerfully, and with depth will help your students succeed in all these endeavors.

We often think of writing as a way of expressing our thoughts, and it is that. But writing also helps us to think. Often, it is only when we sit down to write out our thoughts that we can truly evaluate how ordered and clear, or how scattered and murky, they really are. Your student may ace a multiple choice or short answer test in early American history, but if they can't write an understandable paper on the causes of the Revolution, chances are they don't really understand those causes.

Too many people today walk around in a fog of unformed thoughts, their opinions a mixture of instinct, emotion, and questionable outside influences. One of the most crucial tasks of any educator is to guide students out of that fog, and one of the most effective tools for doing so is to improve their writing. Writing well is an active, forceful method for battling poor thinking.

Many modern programs focus exclusively on getting students to enjoy writing, and I do believe it's important for students to enjoy writing, because we stop doing what we don't enjoy as soon as we can. I also believe, however, that we are much more likely to enjoy what we do well than what we do poorly. Other programs focus solely on the content of the writing, having students write only on topics of philosophical or sociological interest, for example. But if a student can't say something well, it doesn't much matter what they say, because no one will take them seriously. So, rather than giving you *101 Ways To Make Writing More Fun* or *World Views in Literature*, I try here to give your student ways to make their writing more powerful, more persuasive, and more entertaining.

When your student completes a composition that truly hits the mark, it will be more than fun, it will be exhilarating. And when your student can write effectively about a character in a story or meter in a poem, they will be able to write effectively about anything.

Weekly Planning Schedule

Note that comprehension questions are not mentioned in the following lesson planner. Please see Comprehension Questions on page 2 of this Guide and plan accordingly. The following schedule assumes that comprehension questions will be completed along with the reading at the pace that you choose (daily, weekly, bi-weekly, etc.). Comprehension questions are located in the student guide immediately following the vocabulary for each reading selection. Answers are in this Guide with each chapter.

Note that in the second semester there are more comprehension questions per week, on average, than in the first. This gives students more challenge as they progress through the class. If you need to, don't hesitate to test more frequently in the second semester than you did in the first.

This schedule does not take into account any vocabulary, grammar, or other language-arts work you may be doing. Because this varies from family to family, I decided to create a weekly rather than daily schedule. You may choose, for example, to do only literature on Mondays, Wednesday, and Fridays and only grammar and vocabulary on Tuesdays or Thursdays. Others may wish to work on all subjects, all days. This schedule allows for both.

There is no harm in letting students who finish early with a week's worth of work to work ahead, This may give some breathing room later if they find they need more time than allotted with a later lesson, or they can take the extra time to write extra compositions. One full week is allotted at the end for any catch-up work that is necessary and to review all papers written during the semester.

All references to the Lightning Lit Guide in this schedule refer to the Student Guide. You should grade the assigned work as it is completed.

Semester 1

WEEK 1

M ☑ Read "Welcome to Lightning Literature," p. 1.

M ☑ Read *Lightning Lit*, Chapter 1, "Introduction," pp. 5–6.

M ☑ Read "A Crazy Tale," pp. 28–33 in *Stories and Poems for Extremely Intelligent Children*.

W ☐ Read *Lightning Lit* Chapter 1, lesson and mini-lesson, pp. 8–18.

M–F ☐ Complete as many workbook pages as possible for "A Crazy Tale," pp. 1–18 (in back of the student guide).

WEEK 2

M–F ☐ Finish any remaining workbook pages for "A Crazy Tale."

M–F ☐ Complete one writing lesson for "A Crazy Tale," pp. 19–20; if you finish this early, you may complete a second writing exercise.

WEEK 3

☐ Review composition(s) for "A Crazy Tale" and make any necessary revisions.

☐ Read *Lightning Lit*, Chapter 2, "Introduction," pp. 23–24.

☐ Read Chapters 1–12 of *Treasure Island*, pp. 3–105.

WEEK 4

☐ Read Chapters 13–27 of *Treasure Island*, pp. 109–232.

WEEK 5

☐ Read Chapters 28–34 of *Treasure Island*, pp. 235–298.

☐ Read *Lightning Lit* Chapter 2, lesson and mini-lesson, pp. 34–45.

☐ Complete as many workbook pages as possible for *Treasure Island*, pp. 19–40 (in back of the student guide).

WEEK 6

☐ Finish any remaining workbook pages for *Treasure Island*.

☐ Complete one writing exercise for *Treasure Island*, pp. 46–47; if you finish this early, you may complete a second writing exercise.

WEEK 7

☐ Review composition(s) for *Treasure Island* and make any necessary revisions.

☐ Read *Lightning Lit*, Chapter 3, "Introduction," pp. 51–52.

☐ Read all poems for this lesson from *Stories and Poems*:
"There Was a Child Went Forth" by Walt Whitman
—pp. 40–42
"I Saw a Peacock with a Fiery Tail"—anonymous—p. 127
"The Mad Gardener's Song" by Lewis Carroll—pp. 149–150
"The War-Song of Dinas Vawr" by Thomas Love Peacock—pp. 150–152
"The Dalliance of the Eagles" by Walt Whitman—p. 348
"London Snow" by Robert Bridges—pp. 417–418

☐ Read *Lightning Lit*, Chapter 3, lesson and mini-lesson, pp. 55–63

☐ Complete as many workbook pages as possible for Vivid Imagery in Poetry, pp. 41–63 (in back of the student guide).

WEEK 8

☐ Finish any remaining workbook pages for Vivid Imagery in Poetry.

☐ Complete one writing exercise for Vivid Imagery in Poetry, pp. 64–65; if you finish this early, you may complete a second writing exercise.

WEEK 9

☐ Review composition(s) for Vivid Imagery in Poetry and make any necessary revisions.

☐ Read *Lightning Lit*, Chapter 4, "Introduction," p. 69.

☐ Read Chapters 1–6 of *A Day of Pleasure*, pp. 5–71.

WEEK 10

☐ Read Chapters 7–12 of *A Day of Pleasure*, pp 77–147.

WEEK 11

☐ Read Chapters 13–19 of *A Day of Pleasure*, pp 153–227.

☐ Read *Lightning Lit*, Chapter 4, lesson and mini-lesson, pp. 78–86.

☐ Complete as many workbook pages as possible for *A Day of Pleasure*, pp. 65–84 (in back of the student guide).

WEEK 12

☐ Finish any remaining workbook pages for *A Day of Pleasure*.

☐ Complete one writing exercise for *A Day of Pleasure*, pp. 87–88; if you finish this early, you may complete a second writing exercise.

WEEK 13

❏ Review composition(s) for *A Day of Pleasure* and make any necessary revisions.
❏ Read *Lightning Lit*, Chapter 5, "Introduction," pp. 91–92.
❏ Read "Wakefield" from *Stories and Poems*, pp. 254–261.
❏ Read *Lightning Lit*, Chapter 5, lesson and mini-lesson, pp. 95–109
❏ Complete as many workbook pages as possible for "Wakefield," pp. 85–115 (in back of the student guide).

WEEK 14

❏ Finish any remaining workbook pages for "Wakefield"
❏ Complete one writing exercise for "Wakefield," pp. 110–111; if you finish this early, you may complete a second writing exercise

WEEK 15

❏ Review composition(s) for "Wakefield" and make any necessary revisions.
❏ Read *Lightning Lit*, Chapter 6, "Introduction," pp 115–116.
❏ Read Chapters 1–3 of *A Christmas Carol*, pp. 1–91.

WEEK 16

❏ Read Chapters 4–5 of *A Christmas Carol*, pp. 92–126.
❏ Read *Lightning Lit*, Chapter 6, lesson and mini-lesson, p. 125-132.
❏ Complete as many workbook pages as possible for *A Christmas Carol*, pp. 117–140 (in back of the student guide).

WEEK 17

❏ Finish any remaining workbook pages for *A Christmas Carol*.
❏ Complete one writing exercise for *A Christmas Carol*, pp. 133–134; if you finish this early, you may complete a second writing exercise.

WEEK 18

❏ Review all the writing exercises you've completed so far and make any necessary changes.

Semester 2

WEEK 1

❏ Read *Lightning Lit*, Chapter 7, "Introduction," pp. 137–138.

❏ Read all poems for this lesson from *Stories and Poems*:
"Goblin Market" by Christina Rossetti—pp. 264–279
"A Leave-Taking" by Algernon Charles Swinburne—pp. 315–316
"Autumn" by John Clare—pp. 317–318
"Weep You No More, Sad Fountains" by Anonymous—p. 322
"Love Will Find Out the Way" by Anonymous —pp. 352–353
"Who Has Seen the Wind?" by Christina Rossetti—p. 358
"The Silver Swan" by Orlando Gibbons—p. 381
"The Snowstorm" by Ralph Waldo Emerson—p. 416

❏ Read *Lightning Lit* Chapter 7, lesson and mini-lesson, pp. 142–150

❏ Complete as many workbook pages as possible for Figurative Language. pp. 141–161 (in back of the student guide).

WEEK 2

❏ Finish any remaining workbook pages for Figurative Language.

❏ Complete one writing lesson for Figurative Language pp. 151–152; if you finish this early, you may complete a second writing exercise.

WEEK 3

❏ Review composition(s) for Figurative Language and make any necessary revisions.

❏ Read *Lightning Lit*, Chapter 8, "Introduction," pp. 155–156.

❏ Read Chapters I–VI of *The Hobbit*, pp. 1–111.

WEEK 4

❏ Read Chapters VII–XII of *The Hobbit* pp. 112–233.

WEEK 5

❏ Read Chapters XIII–XIX of *The Hobbit* pp. 234–305.

❏ Read *Lightning Lit* Chapter 8, lesson and mini-lesson, pp. 165–174.

❏ Complete as many workbook pages as possible for *The Hobbit*, pp. 163–185 (in back of the student guide).

WEEK 6

❏ Finish any remaining workbook pages for *The Hobbit*.

❏ Complete one writing exercise for *The Hobbit*, pp. 175–176; if you finish this early, you may complete a second writing exercise.

WEEK 7

☐ Review composition(s) for *The Hobbit* and make any necessary revisions.
☐ Read *Lightning Lit*, Chapter 9, "Introduction," p. 179.
☐ Read "Reflections" from *Stories and Poems* pp. 42–48.
☐ Read *Lightning Lit*, Chapter 9, lesson and mini-lesson, pp. 181–187.
☐ Complete as many workbook pages as possible for "Reflections," pp. 187–210 (in back of the student guide).

WEEK 8

☐ Finish any remaining workbook pages for "Reflections."
☐ Complete one writing exercise for "Reflections," pp. 188–189; if you finish this early, you may complete a second writing exercise.

WEEK 9

☐ Review composition(s) for "Reflections" and make any necessary revisions.
☐ Read *Lightning Lit*, Chapter 10, "Introduction," pp. 193–194.
☐ Read the Preface–Chapter 8 of *My Family and Other Animals*, pp. xi–109. **NOTE:** This book contains mild swearing. You may want to read the book first and eliminate certain sections from your child's assigned reading or talk about it with you child.

WEEK 10

☐ Read Chapters 9–15 of *My Family and Other Animals*, pp. 110–220.

WEEK 11

☐ Read Chapters 16 through "The Return" of *My Family and Other Animals*, pp. 220–273.
☐ Read *Lightning Lit*, Chapter 10, lesson and mini-lesson, pp. 204–214.
☐ Complete as many workbook pages as possible for *My Family and Other Animals*, pp. 211–230 (in back of the student guide).

WEEK 12

☐ Finish any remaining workbook pages for *My Family and Other Animals*.
☐ Complete one writing exercise for *My Family and Other Animals*, pp. 215–216; if you finish this early, you may do a second writing exercise.

WEEK 13

☐ Review composition(s) for *My Family and Other Animals* and make any necessary revisions.

- [ ] Read *Lightning Lit*, Chapter 11, "Introduction," pp. 219–220.
- [ ] Read all poems for this lesson from *Stories and Poems*:
  "The Human Seasons" by John Keats—p. 25
  "The Fairies" by William Allingham—pp. 52–53
  "I Loved a Lass" by George Wither—pp. 345–346
  "The Splendour Falls on Castle Walls" by Alfred, Lord
    Tennyson—pp. 346–347
  "So, We'll Go No More A-Roving" by G. Gordon, Lord Byron—pp. 347–348
  "A Wintry Sonnet" by Christina Rossetti—p. 380
  "Nightmare" by William Schwenk Gilbert—pp. 382–384
  "Mariana" by Alfred, Lord Tennyson—pp.512–515
- [ ] Read *Lightning Lit*, Chapter 11, lesson and mini-lesson, pp. 224–236.
- [ ] Complete as many workbook pages as possible for Meter in Poetry
  pp. 231–249 (in back of the student guide).

WEEK 14

- [ ] Finish any remaining workbook pages for Meter in Poetry.
- [ ] Complete one writing exercise for Meter in Poetry pp. 237–238; if you finish
  this early, you may complete a second writing exercise.

WEEK 15

- [ ] Review composition(s) for Meter in Poetry and make any necessary revisions.
- [ ] Read *Lightning Lit*, Chapter 12, "Introduction," pp. 241–242.
- [ ] Read Chapters 1–15 of *To Kill a Mockingbird*, pp. 3–155.
  NOTE: This book contains mild swearing. You may want to
  read the book first and eliminate certain sections from your
  child's assigned reading or talk about it with you child.

WEEK 15

- [ ] Read *Lightning Lit*, Chapter 12, lesson and mini-lesson, pp. 254–265.
- [ ] Read Chapters 16–31 of *To Kill a Mockingbird*, pp. 155–281.
- [ ] Complete as many workbook pages as possible for *To Kill a Mockingbird*,
  pp. 253–279 (in back of the student guide).

WEEK 17

- [ ] Finish any remaining workbook pages for *To Kill a Mockingbird*.
- [ ] Complete one writing exercise for *To Kill a Mockingbird*, p. 266; if you finish
  this early, you may complete a second writing exercise.

WEEK 18

- [ ] Review all the writing exercises you've completed this semester (or for the
  entire year if you prefer) and make any necessary changes.

Congratulations on finishing this course!

Chapter One

"A Crazy Tale" by G. K. Chesterton

Stories and Poems for Extremely Intelligent Children of All Ages
    —Pages 28 to 33

Student Guide—Pages 3 to 20

Workbook—Pages 1 to 18

Chapter 1: "A Crazy Tale"

Answers to Comprehension Questions

1. He says he knew there had been a creation of a second Adam.
2. This is how the man describes grass.
3. The man is talking about the sun.
4. The man describes his parents as giants.
5. He says he hears the daisies growing.
6. Being born was the greatest event of the man's life.
7. The man says his function is thanking God for his creation.
8. The man describes his feet in this manner.
9. The narrator decides the man is mad.

Literary Lesson: Author's Purpose

Identifying an author's purpose in nonfiction writing tends to be easier than in fiction, but as we encounter nonfiction writing every day, it is also very important. Take the time on a regular basis to read newspaper and magazine articles with your student and discuss the author's purpose. Although many are meant to inform, many are also meant to persuade; and it can be particularly important to discern the difference between these two. Learning this will help students recognize when they are genuinely being informed of facts and when the author has a particular bias that he or she wishes to put across as fact (though it is actually opinion).

Identifying an author's purpose in fiction tends to be more complex, and if the student has trouble with it in this one lesson, don't worry too much. The idea is brought up again in future lessons. Students who wish to try again with a different story, though, may read "How Much Land Does a Man Need?" by Leo Tolstoy (p. 298 of *Stories and Poems*). After they've read it, ask if they can discern the author's purpose, that is, Tolstoy's message. (Tolstoy's purpose is to communicate the idea that the only land men need to own is that which they will be buried in.) If they cannot, tell them that Tolstoy did not believe in ownership of private property. Then look through the story together to see what clues are in the story itself that express this idea.

If you have an advanced student, another activity you could do to expand this lesson is to read Thornton Wilder's play *Our Town* together (it is a brief play).

It is available from most libraries. *Our Town* has a similar purpose as Chesterton's story—to emphasize the importance of appreciating common, everyday things. Wilder achieves his purpose in a very different manner, however. Discuss with the student the differences between these two pieces of literature and how they approach the same purpose in different ways. This could even be the topic of a comparison/contrast paper for the student.

This extra challenge possibility, and others I list throughout the year, can be postponed until the end of this course then done as time allows.

Mini-Lesson: Taking Notes

As I say in the mini-lesson, there are four core ideas to taking notes:

- Know what the topic of your paper is and only take notes pertinent to it.
- When you paraphrase a source, avoid plagiarism.
- When you quote directly from a source, quote accurately and in context.
- Note down all pertinent information for proper citation later.

The rest of the lesson goes into more detail about each of these items. This is a skill that best improves with practice. Students who enjoy research papers will find this no trouble. Students who have never done one, or do them only grudgingly, need to be encouraged to write some this year since it is a vital skill for high school and college. To help the first-time or reluctant students, allow them to choose their own topic. Assign short papers at first and require only two or three sources. (Requiring only one source is a bad idea because it encourages the student to rewrite information from only one source rather than merging the ideas and information from two or more places.) This course provides many opportunities for research papers, but you can also assign them in other classes like history, science, or even art and music. (See section on mini-lessons on Page 3 of this Guide.)

Writing Exercises

The first exercise is probably the easiest, as it is the shortest. Some students will be drawn to the creativity of it, while others will not like it (particularly if they did not like the story). It does not directly address the lesson, but may be a good choice for a student who does not like to write or has not written much.

The second exercise directly addresses the lesson, and gives students a chance to use one of their workbook pages as well. This is perhaps a better choice for the student who is uneasy with writing but doesn't want to do something more creative such as the first selection. If they reuse their two paragraphs from the workbook pages, they need only write three more.

The third exercise addresses the second part of the lesson, on fiction. This is a good choice for students who already like writing short stories or who are eager to start. This exercise may make them more conscious of their writing process in that they need to sculpt the story to communicate their purpose. It also gives them a chance to tie a story directly into their life or beliefs.

The fourth exercise is good for a student who likes research papers or one who needs more practice with research papers and who isn't strongly attracted to one of the other exercises. It is the gentlest of research papers in that students can choose the topic, there is no minimum number of pages required, and they don't even have to worry about citations and a bibliography. It is important that they include their notes though, as this exercise addresses the content of the mini-lessons on note-taking.

Discussion Questions

1. The man with the story said that his purpose was "thanking God for his creation." Do you think he was especially well-suited to this purpose, given his unique way of seeing the world? He also says this is a "new function never before conceived truly." In other words, we've never before really understood how we should thank God for his creation. Do you think that's true?

2. Chesterton believed we should appreciate things. How well do you think you appreciate things, especially the common, every-day things around you? Do you think you can ever appreciate them, or thank God for them, sufficiently? What can you do to increase your appreciation?

Workbook Answers

1.1.L DISCERNING AUTHOR'S PURPOSE (5 POINTS POSSIBLE)

1. The purpose of the paragraph is to **describe**.
2. The purpose of the paragraph is to **inform**.
3. The purpose of the paragraph is to **explore**.
4. The purpose of the paragraph is to **persuade**.
5. The purpose of the paragraph is to **explain/instruct**.

1.2.L WRITING WITH A PURPOSE

Student answers will vary. The important thing here is that each paragraph fulfills the purpose the student says it does.

1.3.G CAPITALIZATION AND APOSTROPHES (47 POINTS POSSIBLE)

George **B**ernard **S**haw was an **I**rishman, born to **P**rotestant parents, though he became an outspoken atheist. **A**theism wasn'**t S**haw'**s** only unusual belief or practice. **H**e was also a vegetarian (more unusual in those days than now, but it may have done his health well, as he lived until age 94), and a radical socialist who believed that land and property should be distributed equally.

It'**s** hard to say which was more important to **S**haw—his politics or his plays. **H**e wrote many of these, perhaps the most famous of which are *Major Barbara* and *Pygmalion.* **B**ut **S**haw'**s** plays are not free of his politics. **I**n fact, they sometimes include lengthy introductions filled with politics. **O**ne needs to have an understanding of **S**haw'**s** socialism to really understand his plays.

Say what you might about **S**haw, he was a witty man. **H**e is famous for such quotes as, "**M**ost people would rather die sooner than think. **I**n fact, they do so" and "**Y**outh is wasted on the young." **I**f someone tells you that you have a "**S**havian wit" it'**s** a compliment—*Shavian* being the adjective form of **S**haw'**s** name.

Shaw'**s** good friend, **G**. **K**. **C**hesterton, said this about him: "**M**ost people say that they agree with **B**ernard **S**haw or that they do not understand him. **I** am the only person who understands him, and **I** do not agree with him." **S**haw was often hard to understand, and even harder to agree with; but his writing has endured, and he is still a fascinating read.

The primary purpose of these paragraphs is to inform.

1.4.T FACT AND OPINION (8 POINTS POSSIBLE)

G. K. Chesterton was not a communist, socialist, or capitalist. Instead, he and a friend named Hilaire Belloc formulated a new economic system called *distributism.* <u>Distributism is a fascinating system.</u>

In communism all businesses and resources (formally called "means of production") are owned by the government. In socialism, only some means of production are controlled by the state. In capitalism, people, rather than the government, control businesses; but usually it is only a few people rather than many. <u>Distributism is better than all these ways.</u>

In distributism, the means of production would be distributed among all the people. Everyone would own a small parcel of land (rather than a few people owning much land and many people owning none). Distributism also emphasizes small-scale production such as small farmers and craftspeople rather than large-scale production in factories. Distributists believe these practices will help keep families together (the sacredness of family is very important in distributism) and make people feel more connected to their work. <u>Chesterton and Belloc were brilliant men, and they devised an economic system that would make the world a better place. Distributism would be healthy for families and would preserve people's dignity and elevate the human spirit better than communism, socialism, or capitalism. Distibutism is the way of a brighter future.</u>

1. The primary purpose of the paragraphs is to persuade. (Some students may say the primary purpose is to inform. Although these paragraphs do also inform, that is not their primary purpose.)

2. Yes, the writer of these paragraphs has a bias.

3. The writer is biased in favor of distributism (or against communism, socialism, and capitalism). The writer is also biased in favor of Chesterton and Belloc, though that is secondary.

1.5.M Taking Notes

Answers will vary somewhat, but students should have notes from all three sources. Each source should also contain full information:

> "Shaw for Better or Worse" by Margo Sturgis in a magazine entitled *Luck of the Irish* (issue 5, number 9, pages 32–36).

> Arthur Bailey, *Distributism Facts and Fallacies*. The website address is www.distributismisforyou.com. (This entry should also have a date for when the student took down the information.)

> Elizabeth Kamath, *Lightning Literature and Composition*, Grade 8, pages 5–6. Published by Hewitt Homeschooling Resources, 2006, Washougal, WA.

Be sure all notes pertain to the topic, a comparison and contrast paper on G. K. Chesterton and George Bernard Shaw. Student must also include one quote. Be sure it matches the original source exactly.

1.6.P "A Crazy Tale" Crossword Puzzle

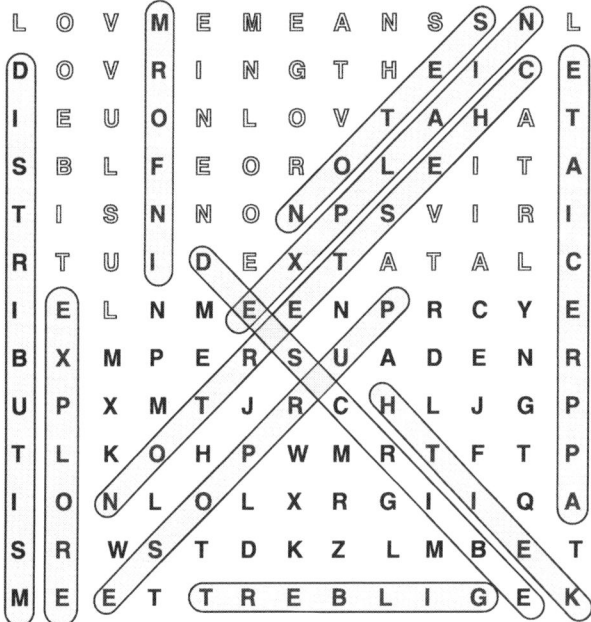

1.7.P "A Crazy Tale" Word Search

1.8.E AUTHOR'S PURPOSE

1. c

2. c

3. e

4. Any of these

5. He saw the humor of how it appears to eat asparagus, and took advantage of the "etiquette" involved in the process.

Chapter Two

Treasure Island by Robert Louis Stevenson

Student Guide—Pages 21 to 47

Workbook—Pages 19 to 40

Chapter 2: *Treasure Island*

Answers to Comprehension Questions

CHAPTER 1

1. Jim thinks the seaman chose their inn because it was well spoken of and because it was described as lonely.
2. He describes the man as a seafaring man with one leg.

CHAPTER 2

1. When Bill first sees Black Dog, he looks like he has seen a ghost.
2. The doctor tells Bill he must stop drinking so much rum.

CHAPTER 3

1. The death of Jim's father distracts him from the captain.
2. It is called "The Black Spot" because that is what the captain receives, and it kills him.

CHAPTER 4

1. The people refuse to return with Jim and his mother because they are afraid of Captain Flint, those who know him, and smugglers.
2. Student answers will vary, but might be something like: The shells were of no practical or monetary value, but were probably beautiful, and to value something like this seems very unlike what we've seen of the captain.
3. Jim and his mother take some guineas (coins) and an oilskin of paper.

CHAPTER 5

1. The pirates' two main concerns are finding Jim and his mother and the approaching danger that Dirk's whistle warns them of. Pew is more concerned with finding Jim and his mother.
2. Pew is killed when one of the revenue officer's horses tramples him.

CHAPTER 6

1. The crosses stand for ships or towns that the pirates robbed.
2. Livesey says this because the pirates will do anything to get their hands on the map; and if they find out who has it, their lives will be in danger.

CHAPTER 7

1. He is first upset when he sees the boy the squire hired to work for his mother; he finally realizes that he is not just going to sea but leaving home and his mother.

2. The first example of foreshadowing in this chapter is when Jim says, ". . . but in all my fancies nothing occurred to me so strange and tragic as our actual adventures." The second example of foreshadowing is when the squire writes to Livesey and Jim that he has engaged a one-legged sailor to journey with them.

CHAPTER 8

1. Jim thinks Long John Silver is not the man the captain warned him about because Silver is so clean and pleasant.

2. Black Dog is in Silver's tavern.

CHAPTER 9

1. Student must name at least two of the following: (1) The crew knows more about the voyage than he does, (2) the voyage is for treasure, (3) the purpose of the voyage is supposed to be secret but the secret has been told to everyone, (4) he doesn't like the crew, (5) he believes he should have been able to choose his own crew, and (6) Mr. Arrow is too free and familiar with the crew.

2. The captain means the secret has been told to many people.

3. Student must name at least one of the following: The captain wants (1) the powder and arms under the cabin, (2) the squire's own people berthed beside the cabin, (3) to keep the map a secret from everyone including him.

CHAPTER 10

1. The two problems with Mr. Arrow are that he is too familiar with the men and he gets drunk.

2. Long John Silver's nickname is Barbecue.

CHAPTER 11

1. Jim is probably frightened when he hears that Silver sailed under Captain Flint.

2. By a "gentleman of fortune" Silver means a pirate.

3. Silver plans to kill all the honest men after getting the treasure.

CHAPTER 12

1. Captain Smollett hands Silver a copy of the treasure map with the marks for the treasure omitted.
2. The men know they can trust the squire's home servants.

CHAPTER 13

1. Jim's heart sank, and he hated even the thought of Treasure Island when he saw it.
2. The captain allows the men shore leave to delay the threat of mutiny.

CHAPTER 14

1. He is alerted to the approaching people by the ducks flying out of the marsh.
2. Jim sees Long John Silver kill Tom.

CHAPTER 15

1. Ben Gunn was marooned because he had urged his ship to land on the island and the hands searched for the treasure, but they couldn't find it after twelve days of looking.
2. Ben Gunn knew there was treasure on the island because he had been one of Flint's crew when Flint buried it.

CHAPTER 16

1. The stockade has water, which the cabin lacks.
2. The doctor is able to bring a second boatload of supplies to the stockade because he and his men are armed, and the crewmen that have spotted them are not.

CHAPTER 17

1. The doctor and his companions forget the "long nine" gun and its powder and shot.
2. They lose three guns and half their powder and provisions.

CHAPTER 18

1. The captain runs up the British flag.
2. It is a problem to wait until August for help because their supplies will run out before then.

CHAPTER 19

1. Ben Gunn convinces Jim by telling him that the pirates would fly the Jolly Roger, not the British flag.

2. Student must name at least one of the following: (1) the cold breeze blows through the house, (2) there is sand everywhere, (3) there was only a hole in the roof to let the smoke out so most of it stayed in, and (4) Tom's dead body is still in the cabin.

3. Jim says rum and the climate were two of their allies.

CHAPTER 20

1. Silver thinks the captain or one of his men has done the killing, but it was actually Ben Gunn.

2. Student answers will vary, but must be defended well. A good answer would be: The captain makes the right choice because he knows Silver originally intended to kill them all and he has proven to be an untrustworthy man.

CHAPTER 21

There are no questions for this chapter.

CHAPTER 22

1. Jim decides to leave the stockade because he is disgusted by the heat, blood, and filth and wants to walk under the cool trees.

2. Jim decides to take Ben Gunn's boat and cut the *Hispaniola* adrift.

CHAPTER 23

1. The tide takes Jim in his boat to the *Hispaniola*.

2. They don't notice because they are fighting with each other.

CHAPTER 24

1. Jim describes sea lions in this way.

2. Jim decides not to sit up and paddle because when he does so the boat becomes very unstable.

3. Jim comes across the surprising site of the *Hispaniola* under sail and decides to board her.

CHAPTER 25

1. Jim finds Israel Hands alive.

2. They agree that Hands will tell Jim how to navigate the ship to land if Jim feeds Hands and binds his wound.

CHAPTER 26

1. Israel tells Jim he wants him to go to the cabin to get him some wine. His actual reason is to arm himself without Jim seeing.

2. Jim is sure Israel won't attack him right away because Israel wants the boat safely moored and only Jim can do that.

3. The ship suddenly cants forty-five degrees to one side, and this gives Jim the chance to get away.

4. Israel throws his knife and hits Jim in the shoulder.

CHAPTER 27

1. a

2. The parrot calling "Pieces of eight!" makes Jim realize who is actually in the stockade.

CHAPTER 28

1. Long John Silver offers to allow Jim to join him, and Jim tells Silver everything he has done against him.

2. Student answers will vary. A good answer would be: Silver likes Jim, admires his courage, and hopes that Jim will help keep him from being executed by the law.

3. Silver tells Jim that the doctor gave Silver the treasure map.

CHAPTER 29

1. The four charges the men make against Silver and his answers are as follows:

(1) They charge that Silver made a mess of the voyage and getting the treasure. Silver replies that it would have gone smoothly except that three of the men—including one of those now charging him—conspired against him.

(2) They charge that Silver agreed to take over the stockade even though it was obvious the doctor and the others wanted out. Silver says that the men begged him to because they were starving, and that he also did it to get the treasure map (which he shows the men).

(3) They charge that Silver allowed the men to live. Silver replies that they need a doctor to tend to their wounds and illnesses and that the men will be good hostages when the consort arrives.

(4) They charge that Silver is allowing Jim to live. Silver replies that Jim is also a good hostage.

2. Seeing that he has the treasure map changes their minds.

CHAPTER 30

1. He allows the doctor and Jim to talk.

2. The doctor says that about Jim finding Ben Gunn.

CHAPTER 31

1. Student must name at least one of the following: (1) which side Silver will eventually join with, (2) why his friends left the stockade, (3) why his friends gave the treasure map to Silver, and (4) what the doctor's warning about "squalls" meant.

2. The first thing the men find is a skeleton. It is the pointer talked about on the back of the map.

3. The men think Flint's spirit might be nearby because they didn't find any of the dead pirate's belongings alongside his skeleton.

CHAPTER 32

1. The sound of a voice singing "Fifteen men" terrifies the men because they believe it is Flint.

2. They're no longer afraid when they recognize the voice as Ben Gunn's.

3. The men find that someone has already dug up the treasure.

CHAPTER 33

1. The doctor gave the treasure map to Long John Silver because it was useless (since Ben Gunn had already dug up the treasure).

CHAPTER 34

1. They leave the three pirates on the island.

2. Long John Silver steals some of the treasure and flees.

Literary Lesson: Setting

Identifying the time(s) and place(s) a story is set in is usually fairly basic, and most students will have no problem with this. When their attention is drawn to it, they will usually also easily recognize detail in setting, including a variety of sensory detail (sight, sound, taste, smell, touch). Students may still have some trouble recognizing when a setting is doing another job as well, such as developing a character or creating a mood. If your student struggles a bit with this chapter, it would be good to reread this lesson again when you get to Chapter 8 on *The Hobbit*. Read the lesson together before the student reads *The Hobbit* and encourage the student to look for ways that Tolkien uses setting. This is an excellent book for studying setting since Tolkien took great care with his setting and used it in many ways. Also, the lesson for Chapter 8 is on conflict and thus discusses setting again somewhat since one type of conflict is "character versus nature."

Mini-Lesson: Rewriting in Your Own Words

This is a key idea in learning to write well, and though the student should not be pressured to get it perfect right away, it is something that needs to be worked on until the student has a strong grasp of it. These are the guidelines I give students in this mini-lesson:

- You can use terms that are specific to the information you are trying to communicate.

- You can use wording and information that is very common; but if in doubt, do your best to rewrite it or quote it and give a citation.

- You cannot lift a whole sentence from your source unless you quote and cite it.

- You cannot give someone else's opinions and conclusions as your own, even if you rewrite them in your own words (unless you came to the same conclusion before reading your source's conclusion).

- You cannot lift a phrase or sentence that is uncommon, that demonstrates the personality or style of the author, or that expresses an opinion or conclusion.

If the student struggles with this in the workbook pages, practice it throughout the year by having the student rewrite paragraphs taken from nonfiction articles. They could be from newspapers, magazines, or the web. Ideally, students can choose articles on subjects that interest them. This is also an ideal exercise for history, science, art, or music, as these are classes where they will have to someday apply these skills.

Writing Exercises

The first two exercises are similar. They are equal in length and in type. Some students will find it easier to establish a mood with their setting while others will find it more interesting to present the setting as a character. Both challenge the student's creative-writing skills and ability to describe a setting.

The third exercise is more advanced in that the student must write a whole short story. This is a good choice for students who already like writing short stories or who are eager to start. It gives students the chance to incorporate what they've learned about setting into an entire piece.

The fourth exercise is good for a student who likes research papers or one who needs more practice with research papers and who isn't strongly attracted to one of the other exercises, all of which are more creative in nature. It is the gentlest of research papers in that students can choose the topic, there is no minimum number of pages required, and they don't even have to worry about citations and a bibliography. It is important that they include copies of their original sources though, as this exercise addresses the content of the mini-lesson on rewriting in one's own words. Also, students who did not do the research paper for Lesson 1 should attach a copy of their notes so the teacher can see how well they did with the first mini-lesson.

Discussion Questions

1. Jim is sad to leave his home, but happy to go on his adventure. Have you ever had to leave home for a long period of time? How did it feel? Was there both sadness and a sense of adventure to it?

2. Jim at first thinks Long John Silver is a wonderful man, then finds out he is not at all what he thought him to be. Have you ever had this experience with someone? Has someone fooled you by making you think they were nice or dependable when they turned out not to be at all? Conversely, have you thought badly of someone at first then discovered you were mistaken? How did you feel in either case? What is your opinion of first impressions?

3. Jim does several brave things in this story. Which do you think is the bravest? Why?

4. When Jim sneaks out and ends up regaining the *Hispaniola*, he does something wrong but a great good comes of it in the end. Do you think Jim was right in what he did? Have you ever done something you shouldn't have, only to have good come from it? Do you think that a good result justifies the initial action?

5. Several people in this story take terrible risks or do terrible things, all in order to secure a fortune. Who today takes terrible risks or does terrible things for money? What do you think of these people? What is worth doing for money? How much money is enough?

Workbook Answers

2.1.L ANALYZING SETTING (19 POINTS POSSIBLE)

1. This story is set in the future.

2. The author probably set the story in the future to warn readers about the present. The warning appears to be about over-population.

3. This story is set in 1765.

4. This scene is set at night.

5. This scene is set in Blackmoor Woods.

6. The setting is meant to convey an ominous or frightening mood.

7. "The very trees seemed to reach their bare branches out to snatch me off my seat."

8. This scene is set in a kitchen.

9. The words *cinnamon, chocolate, coffee,* and *roses* address smell.

10. The words *cool, smooth, warm,* and *sponginess* address touch.

11. The words *lemon* and *blueberries* address taste.

12. The mood established by this setting is one of coziness or comfort.

2.2.L DETAIL IN SETTING

Student answers will vary. Encourage students to be as specific with their answers as possible. For example, if student just writes *chair* ask what type of chair, or what color, or what it's made from. They need not go into a long description of each thing, but *leather recliner* or *wooden rocking chair* is sufficient.

2.3.L SAME SETTING; DIFFERENT TIME

Student answers will vary. Encourage students to be as specific with their answers as possible. For example, if your student just writes *chair* ask what type of chair, or what color, or what it's made from. The student need not go into a long description of each thing, but *leather recliner* or *wooden rocking chair* is sufficient. Has the student discovered some variety in the setting based on the various times? What things were different? What things were not different? There are no right or wrong answers here, but these exercises are meant to increase students' observational powers and their attention to detail.

2.4.T IDENTIFYING BIAS (17 POINTS POSSIBLE)

You might have thought that pirates of the seventeenth and eighteenth century were all men. This would be expected, since pirating was a hard, cruel business; and women of that time had no rights but were expected and encouraged to be dependent and ladylike. In fact, it was considered bad luck for a woman to be on board a ship at all. But <u>two remarkable women</u> were pirates in the eighteenth century, and even served together on the same ship.

Anne Bonny (née Cormac) was born sometime in the late seventeenth century in Ireland, though her family soon moved to America. Anne was always a tomboy, much to her father's dismay; but <u>her take-charge attitude served them both well</u> when her mother died and, as a teen-ager, Anne had to manage her father's plantation. Her fierce temper and <u>fighting abilities</u> were also clear at a young age. When a man tried to assault her, <u>she responded well</u> by beating him so severely that he had to spend the next several weeks in bed, recuperating. She was fourteen years old.

Anne's father disowned her two years later when she married a small-time pirate named James Bonny. James didn't make much of a go at it as a pirate though, so he turned to the more lucrative (for him) profession of informing on pirates. Possibly for this reason, Anne left him. After all, many of her friends were pirates, and this was the life of adventure she was drawn to. <u>Perhaps she rightly felt that she was too good for someone who was both incompetent and disloyal.</u>

She soon met her perfect match in a pirate with the delicious name of Calico Jack (Jack Rackham). Jack was handsome and dashing, and more importantly not concerned about the superstitions of women aboard ships. His crew did not feel that way, however, so Anne disguised herself as a man and was part of the crew. Eventually Anne became pregnant, so her secret was out; but by that time <u>she had proven herself by fighting just as heartily as all the men</u>, and they were not interested in crossing her. <u>Sadly, she lost the baby (in spite of going ashore to care for her health), and she then returned to pirating</u>.

Once, after encountering and defeating another ship, some of its crew joined Calico Jack's. Anne became intrigued by one member in particular, and it wasn't long before she discovered Mary Read, yet another woman in disguise as a man. As the only two women pirates on board (or possibly anywhere), they soon became close friends. Calico Jack, thinking Mary was a man, became jealous and confronted them, and Mary revealed that she was a woman. Jack didn't mind two women aboard ship any more than one.

Mary was born at about the same time as Anne, though in England. Unlike Anne, her mother actually raised her as a boy, though the reasons for this are unclear. For a while Mary joined the British military (still disguised as a man, of course), where she fell in love with a fellow soldier. She revealed her true sex, and they were happily married until he died. Mary returned to life as a man and began sailing, when she was captured by Calico Jack's ship.

Mary was just as fierce a pirate as Anne. Once, when a large brute of a pirate threatened to kill a young sailor they had captured (and with whom Mary was in love), Mary bravely challenged the brute to a duel. They went ashore and both missed with their pistols. Armed with cutlasses, Mary was brilliant, dodging, dancing, and surprising the other pirate, and eventually winning the duel, nearly cutting her opponent's head off in the process. Apparently the young sailor was impressed, for they were soon married.

Sadly, these two magnificent women's careers as pirates were cut short. All of the men aboard ship were drunk when they were stopped and boarded by the authorities. Mary and Anne fought valiantly, but even these two women were not enough to defend the ship alone against such a force. All members of the crew were sentenced to hang, but Mary and Anne had their sentences delayed because they were both pregnant. Sadly, Mary died of an illness in prison. Somehow, Anne was set free, but it is not known what happened to her after this. She may have gone back to her father, possibly even back to her husband. But I like to think that she kept her old fighting spirit and went back to the sea.

1. The author's primary purpose is to inform.
2. The author's secondary purpose is to persuade.
3. The author is biased in favor of Anne and Mary.
4. See the underlined portions, above. Student may have more underlined portions than I have. For cxample, a student may underline a whole sentence where I have only underlined a word or phrase, and that is fine. But some students may underline words that are judgments about something other than Mary and Anne (such as calling Calico Jack's name "delicious") and these answers would be wrong.

2.5.M REWRITING SOURCE MATERIAL

Student answers will vary. Just be sure that proper notes are taken and the information is properly rewritten.

2.6.M REWRITING SOURCE MATERIAL

Student answers will vary. Just be sure that proper notes are taken and the information is properly rewritten.

2.7.A ANALYZING LITERATURE (13 POINTS POSSIBLE)

1. The setting for this scene is summer, sometime during the day, in a painter's studio in London. (3 points)

2. Student must name at least three of the following: (1) roses, (2) lilac, (3) pink-flowering thorn, (4) cigarette smoke, (5) laburnum, and (6) woodbine. Another acceptable line of answers would be anything commonly found in a painter's studio that gives off an odor such as oil paints and turpentine. Though these things are not explicitly mentioned, since this is a painter's studio, their presence is a reasonable assumption.

3. The sullen murmur of bees and the dim roar of London.

4. The most likely importance of this setting is that this is the studio where the picture of Dorian Gray was or will be painted.

5. The three possible subjects for the work of art mentioned are (1) Dorian Gray, (2) Lord Henry Wotton, and (3) Basil Hallward. Students' answers will vary on which they think more likely, but they should give a good reason when answering why. For example, a student might say it is most likely Dorian Gray's picture since that is the subject of this story. Another student might say it is most likely Lord Henry's picture and he is there to pose for it.

2.8.P *TREASURE ISLAND* CROSSWORD PUZZLE

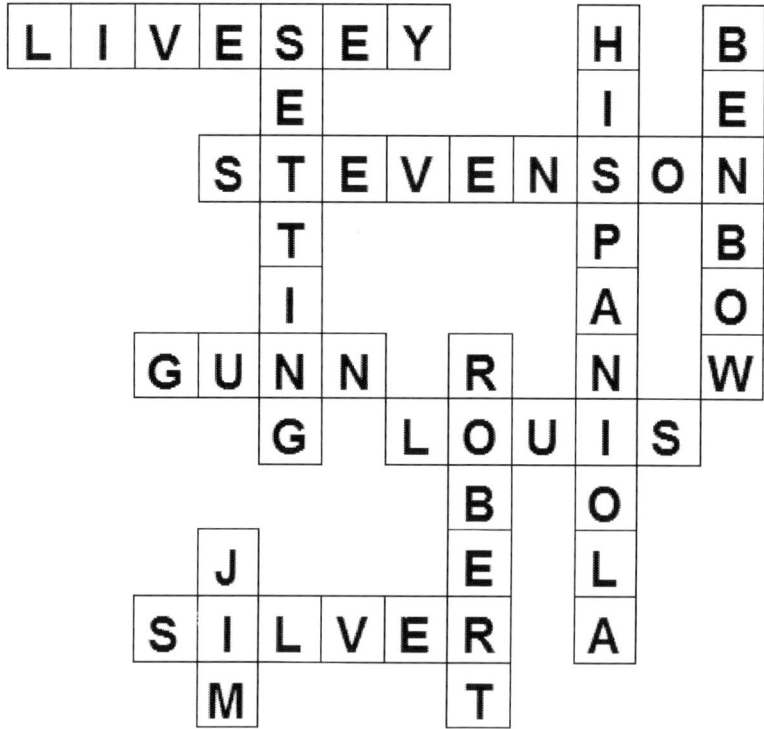

2.9.P *Treasure Island* Word Search

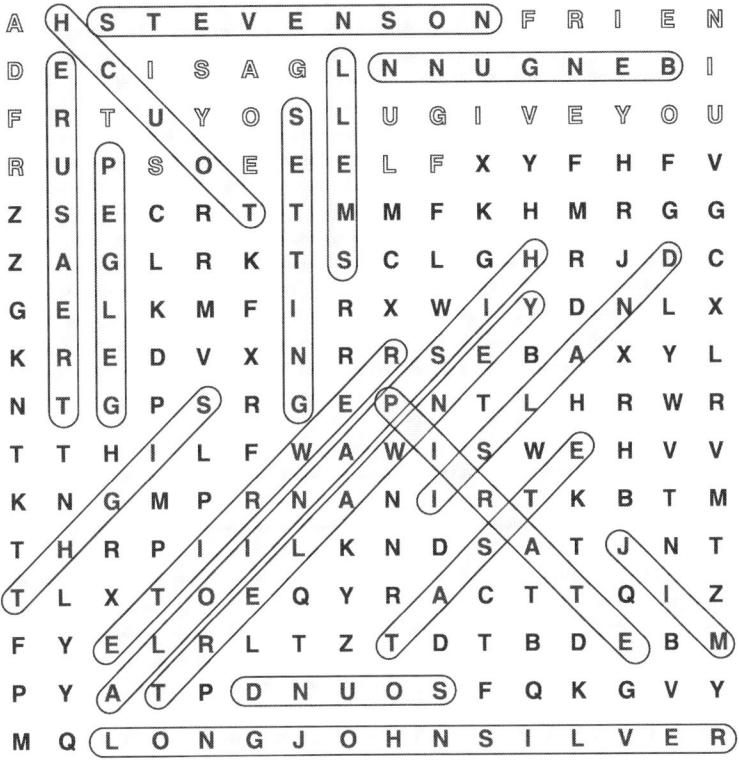

2.10.E Morning Break Fast

Answers will vary but the poem should paint a vivid picture.

Chapter Three

Vivid Imagery in Poetry

Stories and Poems for Extremely Intelligent Children of All Ages

Chapter 3: Vivid Imagery in Poetry

NOTE: If your student did not complete the Grade-7 Lightning Literature guide, be sure he or she is familiar with the following concepts before tackling this chapter:

- **Stanza** A stanza is like a paragraph in poetry. They are usually apparent from line spaces in between them. For example, "The Mad Gardener's Song" has nine stanzas.

- **Rhyme** We mark rhymes in poetry by using letters. When two lines rhyme with each other they are given the same letter. If a line does not rhyme with anything else, it is represented by an *x*. For example, the rhyme scheme of "The Mad Gardener's Song" is *x a x a x a*. The rhyme scheme of "I Saw a Peacock With a Fiery Tail" is *a a b b c c d d e e f f.* Another way to describe this rhyme scheme is to say it is written in couplets (two lines next to each other that rhyme).

Answers to Comprehension Questions

"THERE WAS A CHILD WENT FORTH"
1. The child became the first object he looked upon.
2. Answers for this are too extensive to list. Check your student's answers against the poem itself.

"I SAW A PEACOCK WITH A FIERY TAIL"
There are no comprehension questions for this poem.

"THE MAD GARDENER'S SONG"
There are no comprehension questions for this poem.

"THE WAR-SONG OF DINAS VAWR"
1. They decide to carry off the valley sheep because those sheep were fatter.
2. The second thing the army captures is a herd of cattle.
3. They defeat Ednyfed, king of Dyfed.

"THE DALLIANCE OF THE EAGLES"

1. There are two eagles in this poem.

2. b

"LONDON SNOW"

1. This poem is set in London.

2. The people wake early because the white snow has made it very bright outside.

3. a

Literary Lesson: Vivid Imagery in Poetry

Most students have no trouble identifying imagery in poetry, but some may have trouble putting good imagery in their own writing. If your student has trouble coming up with specific images, it may help to play this game. Name a general category, then each of you take turns listing specific examples of it. (You can play this with as many students as you want, or if you have several students you may want to break up into groups, especially if there are varying abilities. If you have only one student, you should take turns with the student in naming things.) Whoever comes up with the last one wins and gets to name the next general category. This is a particularly good game to play if your student doesn't do well with workbook pages 3.1.L, 3.2.L, and 3.3.L. Here's an example:

> Teacher: Our general category is plants.
> Student 1: rose
> Student 2: orchid
> Student 1: pine tree
> Student 2: dandelion

This goes on until one student is stumped. Let's say it's student 2. In this case, student 1 would get to pick the next general category.

If you wish, you may give hints to keep the players going, especially if they get stumped after only a few efforts. For example, if the students only named flowers at first, you could remind them that trees are also plants.

Depending on the skill level of the student you may want to make the categories more or less general. For example, an exceptionally challenged student may need a very broad category like "animals." But as the student gets better, you can narrow the category to such things as "birds," "farm animals," "pets," "dog breeds." You want to find a category that allows for about five—ten minutes of play. If the student is stumped too soon, he or she will get frustrated; but if the play goes on for too long (and you are one of the participants), you will go quite mad.

For the advanced student who wants to play, you can require that the examples go in alphabetical order. For example:

> Teacher: Our category is birds.
> Student: Albatross
> Teacher: Blue Jay
> Student: Cardinal
> Teacher: Dove

If the student needs or wants more practice identifying and analyzing imagery in poems, choose any poems in *Stories and Poems* (or any book). Some will have more imagery than others, but even poems lacking in a great deal of imagery can teach a lot about it, either because they do have an image that really stands out or because the lack of imagery makes them less interesting to the student. It is also possible that a poem lacking in imagery is appealing to the student. In this case, ask why. What other elements are present in the poem that make it work?

Mini-Lesson: Free Verse and the Ballad

Free Verse can stump some students (and even some adults). We've been trained from an early age that poetry means rhyme. Also, even though many people don't know the terminology or can express what they're hearing in words, we do usually notice meter in poetry and note when it's absent. Therefore, to many people, free verse is just prose with funny line-breaks.

It's not important that students master free verse. If they're interested, find some more poetry by Whitman (though not all his poetry is free verse). His great poem *Leaves of Grass* is free verse, and sections of it are taught in the Lightning Literature course covering American literature of the mid-late nineteenth century. If you already have this guide, you could read the selections included there. (I don't recommend getting the whole poem because sections of it aren't appropriate for junior-high students.) Another excellent free verse poet is William Carlos Williams.

If your student is still struggling with free verse, review this chapter; and if you own the Grade-7 Lightning Lit Guide, you can also review Chapter 7, "Sound in Poetry." These chapters (and Chapter 7 of this guide on figurative language) teach very important aspects of poetry other than rhyme and meter. Next, read a few free-verse poems together and look for examples of these poetic elements. It's even better if you can copy the poems from a book or make a hard copy of poems found on the web so you can write on the poems themselves.

Many students find ballads fun because they tell stories. You can find some ballads on line. For example, go to wikipedia.org and type in *ballad.* Near the end of the entry is a list of links to several ballads. Another ballad in *Stories and Poems* is "Mariana" by Alfred, Lord Tennyson. For a couple of humorous twists on the ballad, have the student read "The Walrus and the Carpenter" (p. 564 of *Stories and Poems)* and "Jabberwocky" (also by Lewis Carroll—this poem is not in this book, but you can find it on line).

Writing Exercises

The first four exercises are poems, and none is really harder than any other (though the first might be a bit easier). It really depends on what the student is drawn to in poetry. The exercises give the student the choice between a rhyming poem of any type, a nonsense poem, free verse, and a ballad.

The fifth exercise is an opinion paper. Many students love writing poetry, but some absolutely hate it. Though I think it's a good idea for students to write at least a poem or two sometime in their school career, I would never force it on a student who was very unwilling. Therefore, every poetry chapter also has at least one non-poetry writing option.

Discussion Questions

1. What does the idea of becoming what you see mean to you? How are you impacted by what you see? How do you think that should affect what you surround yourself with? Do you think different people are impacted differently, or all we all pretty much the same in this regard?

2. What do you think of "nonsense" whether it is in a story, a poem, or some other form? Does Carroll's nonsense poem appeal to you? Does it frustrate you? Bore you? Can you think of any connections between creating "nonsense" like this and creating other types of stories and poems? Might reading these unexpected images help free your mind to think of new possibilities?

3. "The War-Song of Dinas Vawr" was written to satirize (poke fun at) ballads that glorified war. What do you think of poems, stories, movies, etc., that glorify war? Do you think that war can ever be shown realistically in these ways? Should it be?

4. Have you seen animals interacting in nature in the way Whitman describes the eagles? Not necessarily in exactly the same way, but in a

way that arrested your attention? Do you ever wish you could write about such things so you could communicate the sight and your feelings about it to others?

5. Do you like snowfalls? How well do you think Bridges describes one? Do they make you feel the same feelings in the poem?

Workbook Answers

3.1.L VIVID VERBS (40 POINTS POSSIBLE)

Student answers will vary. Be sure each answer is a verb. For example, I sometimes have students give answers such as *marathon* for *run* or *palace* for *build.* Sample answers:

move:	jump, fidget, shake, nod, wave
fall:	collapse, faint, trip, slip, tumble
walk:	saunter, waddle, trudge, strut, creep
touch:	hit, caress, poke, massage, smack
destroy:	break, twist, bend, rip, crumple
repair:	darn, tape, paste, staple, heal
see:	peer, spy, observe, notice, stare
build:	construct, glue, sew, compose, whip up

3.2.L VIVID NOUNS (40 POINTS POSSIBLE)

Student answers will vary. Be sure each answer is a noun. For example, I sometimes have students give answers such as *fly* for *bird* or *drive* for *vehicle.* Sample answers:

bird:	penguin, chicken, hummingbird, raven, thrush
zoo animal:	tiger, lion, ring-tailed lemur, orangutan, zebra
building:	sky-scraper, hut, one-room schoolhouse, fire station, grocery store
vehicle:	double-decker bus, cab, Vespa, Mini Cooper, airplane
color:	yellow, scarlet, cerulean blue, yellow ochre, olive
relative:	mother, father, aunt, cousin, sister-in-law
machine:	combine, printer, lever, coffee dispenser, television
reading material:	novel, *Popular Mechanics,* pamphlet, newspaper, birthday card

Notice that some of these answers are more specific than others. For example, *Popular Mechanics* is a specific magazine, therefore more vivid than simply "novel." Either is an acceptable answer, though the more specific the answer, the better. Encourage students to think of ways to make fairly general answers even more specific.

3.3.L Vivid Adjectives (40 points possible)

Student answers will vary. Be sure each answer is an adjective. For example, I sometimes have students give answers such as *apple* for *red* or *ice* for *cold*. Sample answers:

red:	scarlet, crimson, fire-engine red, maroon, burgundy
loud:	shrill, booming, screechy, piercing, clamorous
bad (smell):	putrid, gamy, musty, rotten, rancid
cold:	icy, frigid, brisk, arctic, nippy
big:	huge, tall, obese, monstrous, gargantuan
small:	teeny, wee, short, microcosmic, petite
old:	ancient, antique, mature, withered, decaying
thin:	skinny, willowy, cadaverous, slight, narrow

Note that some of these are verbals, that is, words that are normally verbs but can be used as adjectives (booming, piercing, decaying). I briefly discuss verbals in the lesson, and it is fine for students to use these.

3.4.L Vivid Sentences

Student answers will vary. Be sure the student has used at least some of the words they came up with in pages 3.1.L, 3.2.L, and 3.3.L. Do not grade this page, but discuss with your students which images they like best and why. Do they think some of the images create a certain feeling?

3.5.M Writing Free Verse

Student answers will vary. Be sure there are five things, and the items should be everyday objects or people for your student. The poem should not rhyme. Ask students to explain their choices of line breaks.

3.6.M Writing a Ballad

Student answers will vary. Be sure there are five events and that each seems a possible choice for a ballad. Also, the student must write one stanza with an *a b a b* rhyme scheme, and you should be able to tell the subject of the ballad just from that one stanza.

3.7.G Verbals (34 points possible)

This exercise covers participles and gerunds—two types of verbals. This book is not meant to teach grammar, but this will be a good review for some students. Others will actually be able to learn the concept just from the little it is discussed in this chapter and from doing this exercise.

1. traveling: verb
2. Sailing: noun
3. crying: adjective
4. cooking: adjective
5. cooking: verb
6. Cooking: noun
7. driving: verb
8. barking: adjective
   chasing: verb
9. writing: noun
   composing: noun
   painting: noun
10. smiling: adjective
    chatting: adjective
    planning: verb
    engaging: verb
    golfing: noun

3.8.T Fact and Opinion (12 points possible)

The poet Robert Frost once said, "Writing free verse is like playing tennis with the net down." I couldn't agree more.

<u>Poetry should be just that—poetry.</u> The nursery rhymes we learn as children all have rhyme and meter. <u>Hence, we know from the beginning that poetry should all have at least one of these aspects, and preferably both. If it doesn't, then it isn't poetry.</u>

Rhyme is when two words have the same vowel and consonant ending sounds, such as *cat* and *bat* or *table* and *cable.* Many types of poetry, such as the limerick and the sonnet, have requirements about rhyming pattern. <u>These types of poetry, even the lowly limerick, are far superior to free verse.</u>

Meter is the rhythm of poetry. Like rhyme, there are types of poetry that require a certain meter. <u>It's difficult to write poetry with a strong meter, but that shouldn't stop a poet from doing so.</u>

<u>Meter and rhyme are more than just good ideas, they are necessary for poetry. Poetry without them lacks harmony and beauty. Poets who write in free verse should stop calling themselves poets and instead write stories or essays.</u>

1. The author's primary purpose is to persuade.

2. Yes, the author has a bias.

3. The author's bias is against free verse.

4. Student must name one of the following: (1) The author quotes a famous poet who holds the same opinion; (2) the author states that much poetry contains rhyme and meter.

3.9.A ANALYZING LITERATURE (7 OR 8 POINTS POSSIBLE)

1. This poem takes place in a village.

2. It takes place on a winter evening, ending at ten o'clock.

3. The speaker's walk takes at least a couple of hours because the title of the poem is "Good Hours."

4. Frost makes the cottages seem more like people by describing their "shining eyes."

5. Details that appeal to the sense of sound are the sound of violin and creaking feet.

6. The cottages sport lace curtains.

7. This poem consists of couplets. (If your student has not taken Lightning Lit 7 and you have not previously studied rhyme patterns—especially couplets—you may drop this question.)

3.10.P Vivid Imagery Crossword Puzzle

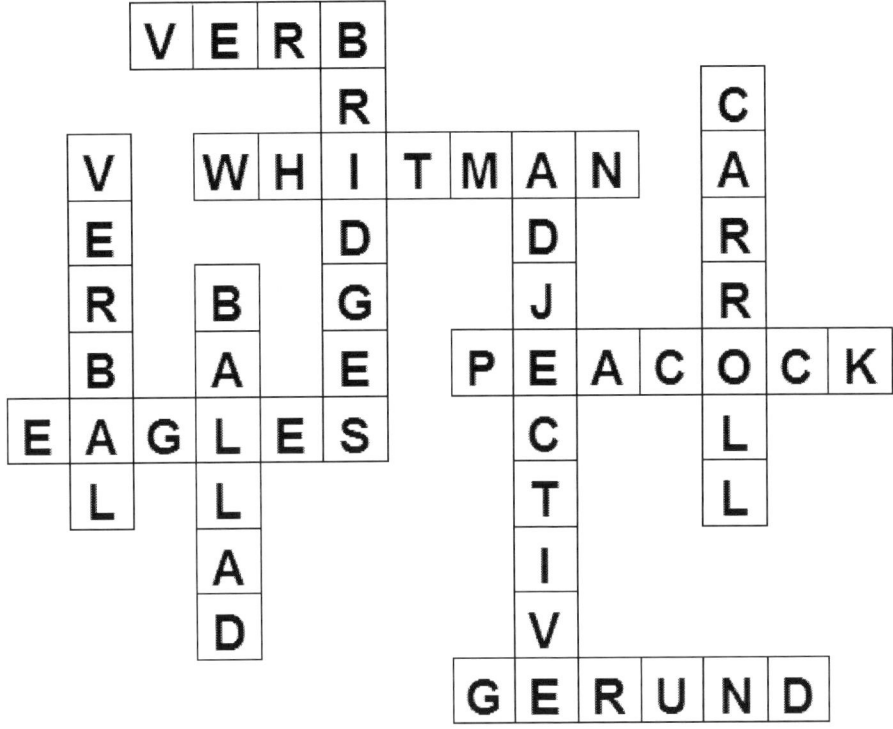

3.11.P Vivid Imagery Word Search

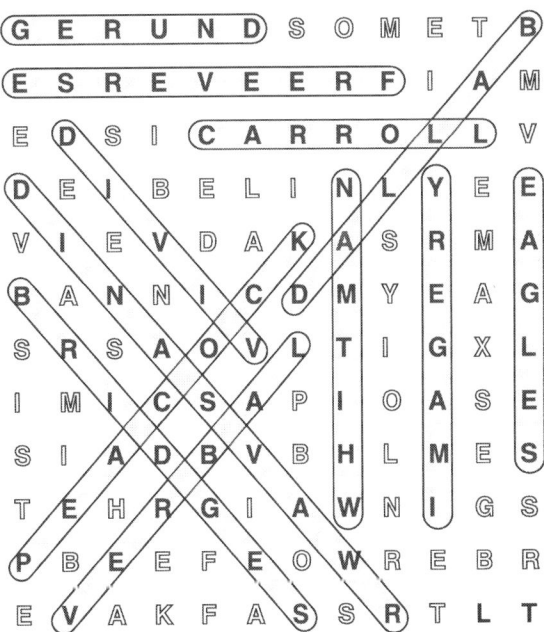

3.12.E CONTENTMENT (33 POINTS POSSIBLE)

Subjects by Stanza: (Words chosen may be different but should be similar in meaning.)

"CONTENTMENT"

1. Home
2. Food
3. Savings/Investments
4. Fame
5. Jewelry
6. Clothing
7. Transportation
8. Paintings
9. Books
10. Possessions
11. Furniture
12. Humility/Simple Tastes/Contentment

"THE WANTS OF MAN"

1. Greed
2. Food
3. Clothing
4. Spouse
5. Children
6. Friend/s
7. Leadership/Fame
8. Good Reputation/Fame
9. Heaven/Mercy

ANSWERS TO QUESTIONS:

1. a

2. Students answers may vary

3. a

4. a

5. Personal tastes would allow for either answer. I would suggest b that Adams is more vivid.

6. b. "The Wants of Man" was written in 1841, and "Contentment" in 1858.

7. Subject, Length, Meter

8. Answers will vary.

9. Answers will vary, but should be supported

Chapter Four

A Day of Pleasure by Isaac Bashevis Singer

Student Guide—Pages 67 to 88

Workbook—Pages 65 to 84

Chapter 4: *A Day of Pleasure*

Answers to Comprehension Questions

CHAPTER 1: WHO I AM

1. The Bible and the Talmud were Singer's only schoolbooks during his early years.

2. Singer writes in Yiddish.

3. Singer says learning was their primary focus ("Our house was a house of learning").

4. The Sabbath was an ordeal for Singer because it is forbidden to write on that day.

5. The family leaves Warsaw because they are starving, so they go to be with his grandparents, where the food is not so scarce.

CHAPTER 2: THE TRIP FROM RADZYMIN TO WARSAW

1. Singer is thrilled about the move from Radzymin to Warsaw.

2. There was a clash between the revolutionaries and the police involving violence.

CHAPTER 3: A DAY OF PLEASURE

1. Singer is afraid his parents will make him spend the ruble on clothes or borrow it and never repay it.

2. Singer first spends his money on a droshky ride, but the man does not take him as far as he paid for.

3. Student must name at least one of the following: (1) Singer eats the candy, (2) he feeds the candy to the swans, (3) he gives a chocolate bar to a little boy, (4) he gives candy to some girls.

4. Student must name at least one of the following: (1) Singer said no blessing before eating the candy, (2) he did not give any of his money to the poor, (3) he had gorged himself. (The student may also list one of the sins Singer later commits on his way home—lying and swearing falsely. These are acceptable answers.)

CHAPTER 4: WHY THE GEESE SHRIEKED

1. Singer's father turns his back because it is forbidden by Jewish law to look at other women.

2. Singer's mother does not believe the dead geese are still shrieking.

3. Their windpipes have not been removed.

CHAPTER 5: REB ASHER THE DAIRYMAN

1. Student must name at least two of the following: (1) Asher was the cantor at Singer's father's services for free, (2) he sent Singer's father the most generous Purim gifts, (3) he lent the Singers money when they could not pay their rent, (4) he gave to charity, (5) he worked 18 hours a day, 6 days a week, yet on the Sabbath studied the Pentateuch, and (6) he respected everyone no matter their age.

2. Singer fears that the horse will take off or that a Gentile will strike him.

3. Asher notices their apartment is on fire, he breaks the door down, wakes them, and smothers the flames.

CHAPTER 6: TO THE WILD COWS

1. Singer gets up early to accompany his friend outside of town to see the wild cows.

2. The Citadel is a prison.

3. Boruch-Dovid tells Singer to take off his boots, but he is embarrassed about walking barefoot.

4. Singer sees timber being shipped by water on rafts.

5. Singer realizes the wild cows and wild man only exist in Boruch-Dovid's imagination.

CHAPTER 7: THE WASHWOMAN

1. The only Gentile in Singer's building is the janitor.

2. The washwoman is much stronger and healthier than the Jewish women of her age.

3. Clothes could not be dried outside because thieves would steal the laundry.

4. The story of the washwoman's faithless son left a deep impression on Singer's mother.

5. The washwoman was delayed in returning their laundry to them because she was ill. Shortly after this, she died.

CHAPTER 8: I BECOME A COLLECTOR

1. Singer becomes a collector for his father because all but one of their previous collectors stole from them, and the family desperately needs money.

2. Singer resolved never to do anything for money that goes against the grain and to avoid favors and presents.

CHAPTER 9: THE STRONG ONES

1. Student must name at least two of the following: (1) bullies, (2) sycophants, (3) "saints" (who weren't really saints), (4) business people, (5) liars, (6) victims.

2. They are close until his friends begin to resent him and grumble about him.

3. Singer says that when one is alone there is nothing to do but study.

4. Singer is angry because his friends want him to plea for a truce even though they were the ones who started the fight.

5. The note says that Singer's friends miss him.

CHAPTER 10: REB ITCHELE AND SHPRINTZA

1. On the Sabbath it is forbidden to cook and to carry money.

2. Singer says that a foreign traveler would have thought of Shprintza as a barbarian.

3. Things were very different at their home on the Sabbath.

4. Every Sabbath the girls would ask Singer which of them he would prefer as his bride. He would always choose the smaller of the two because the other was too big.

5. In these households, Jewishness and worldliness were at odds.

CHAPTER 11: THE MYSTERIES OF THE CABALA

1. They both had a passion for inventing stories.
2. Mendel tells Singer that his family is rich and his father is a robber.
3. Singer tells Mendel that his father is teaching him the Cabala.
4. Mendel tells Singer that he is in love.
5. Singer is sad because he doesn't know who his future wife will be.
6. Singer's father kisses him on his forehead.

CHAPTER 12: THE SATIN COAT

1. Their clothes made their poverty apparent.

2. Before Passover, Singer's father would get commissions for selling to Gentiles the things that Jews could not have in their households during Passover.

3. The study house where they normally go is closed, so they have to go to a different one where nobody knows Singer or cares about his clothes.

CHAPTER 13: A BOY PHILOSOPHER

1. He discusses his views with his mother.

2. Student must name one of the following: Buddha and Confucius.

3. Singer's mother wants him to grow up to be a rabbi.

CHAPTER 14: THE SHOT AT SARAJEVO

1. There were no more newspapers at Singer's home because it was his brother that brought them and his brother had moved out.

2. Student must name at least two of the following: (1) the toilet, (2) the gas oven, (3) the gas meter, (4) the fact that he knew many of the people in the building.

3. The boys decided they wanted Germany to win.

4. The white pins meant that the men had been called up for military service.

5. When Singer's brother was drafted he went into hiding.

6. Shopkeepers began hiding their goods and raising their prices.

7. Singer's father interprets the war as a sign that the Messiah will come soon.

CHAPTER 15: HUNGER

1. The German occupation means that Singer's brother doesn't need to hide from the Russian army any more, so he can come to visit.

2. Singer says the war demonstrated to him that rabbis were unnecessary.

3. Singer says the most difficult thing to bear at this time was the cold.

4. Singer's father endlessly studied the Torah.

CHAPTER 16: THE JOURNEY

1. People were trying to get to Austrian-occupied towns because they had more food than German-occupied towns.

2. Singer is in the cobbler's home when he is overcome with the injustice of the world.

CHAPTER 17: BILGORAY

1. Singer's grandfather (his mother's father) has died.

2. Singer wished he could stay in Bilgoray forever.

CHAPTER 18: THE NEW WINDS

1. Ackerman had a library of worldly books in his house.

2. Singer began to read extensively after their move to Bilgoray.

3. They asked Singer to teach Hebrew.

CHAPTER 19: SHOSHA

1. A house imp lived in Shosha's house and played tricks.

2. When Singer returns to Shosha's home he meets her daughter, Basha.

Literary Lesson: Sharing Your Culture

Discerning information about a culture from fiction or nonfiction can involve quite advanced analysis; this lesson is merely an introduction focusing on some of the more salient aspects. This book is a good one for this purpose, in that Singer gives us information about his culture's values and customs in a clear manner; and that culture is very different from that of most students.

The only way to learn about some cultures is through reading, in part because it would be impossible to actually visit every culture in the world and in part because some cultures no longer exist. Also, even visiting a culture can be less informative than reading about it because a good author can give us more information and a better perspective than we may get on our own, especially if there is a language barrier between us and that culture.

The focus of this lesson is actually more on reading skills than writing, since most people will have more opportunity to read about other cultures than to write about their own. My hope, however, is that by making students aware of ways that authors present cultures in their writing they will gain a deeper understanding of literature. I hope they will also become more astute at understanding all cultures, including their own. This understanding can help students gain new insight into cultures rather than just being subsumed by them.

Mini-Lesson: Rewriting Your Own Words

This is something that students should practice with every paper they write from now until the end of time. I do it myself with all my writing. Many students will find it tedious, but rewriting is crucial for most writers. (I have to be honest and say that there are a handful of great writers who did not rewrite, but they are extremely rare.) If the student finds that they prefer to do the steps in a different order (for example, proofing for grammar and mechanics first), that is fine. I chose the order I prefer, but other orders can work equally well.

Writing Exercises

The first two exercises are similar and allow students to use some information from their workbook pages. The third exercise is probably the hardest, and I would only recommend it for the most advanced students. The one exception is students who have completed the Grade-7 Lightning Lit program. In that case, they will have already read "The Bride Comes to Yellow Sky," and that will make this exercise somewhat easier, since they will not have to read another selection; also this story is one of the easiest for examining culture. The fourth exercise is a research paper. This time I have given topic options. For struggling students who don't like any of these options, feel free to come up with a different research topic. Be sure all aspects of a research paper that have already been addressed in this course are adequately covered in their paper.

Discussion Questions

1. In the first chapter, Singer recalls many questions he started to ask at an early age. When you were younger, did you also ask many questions? Were there particular things that excited your curiosity? If so, what? What kinds of questions did you ask? How did the adults around you respond? Do you wish they had responded differently? If so, how?

2. Singer's father told him that it was not good to indulge in such questions, while his mother told him he would find the answers when he got older. What do you think of these responses? Why do you think his parents said these things? How do you hope to respond to your children someday when they start asking a flurry of questions?

3. Singer gets an unusual amount of money, then spends it in a way that he regrets. Have you ever spent money poorly? Why do you think you did so? When did you decide you had spent it poorly? How did you feel about that? What can you do to prevent that happening again?

4. Several times in the story Singer is subject to discrimination. People look at him with hatred or say cruel things to him because he is Jewish. Have you ever felt discriminated against? For what reason? How did it feel? Have you seen this happen to others? What do you do when you see it happen? What would you like to do if you see it happen in the future?

5. Have you ever encountered a situation—like the shrieking geese—that seemed mysterious or inexplicable at first, only to find a reasonable explanation eventually? What was it? How did it feel when it was mysterious? How did your view of it change after an explanation was found?

6. Have you ever known anyone like Reb Asher—someone who seemed totally good to you? What was that person like?

7. Singer realizes on his outing with his friend Boruch-Dovid that the wild cows and wild man his friend has told him about only exist in his friend's imagination. Was there a time when you suddenly realized something you believed in (maybe Santa Claus or the Tooth Fairy) was only imaginary? How did you feel at that moment? What do you think about people talking about imaginary beings as if they're real? Is it different depending on whether it's a child or an adult doing it? This is a common part of society and of childhood—what function do you think it might serve?

8. Singer says of the washwoman that she "did not want to become a burden, and so she bore her burden." Have you known anyone like this? Do you know people who continue to work hard in spite of their age or failing health? Would you like to be like this when you are older? What can you do throughout life to become this kind of person?

9. Have you ever done something for money that you deeply regretted afterwards, either because it was wrong or because it was just so unpleasant? What criteria do you use for knowing when to do something for money? Must there be some other benefit as well, or is sometimes just getting money enough? Does it depend on how badly you need the money?

10. At the end of Chapter 8, Singer says, "A part of my brain that had been sealed seemed to be opening. I now experienced the profound joy of learning. . ." (94) Have you had this experience? Has there been a time (or times) when you suddenly realized you were understanding something you couldn't understand before—a sort of "A-ha" moment? When was this? How did it feel?

11. In Chapter 9, Singer is very excited about a book his brother brought home (*Crime and Punishment*). When was the first time you were excited about a book? What was the book? Why did it excite you?

12. About this same book, Singer says, "This is no storybook, this is literature." Do you yet have an idea about the difference between literature and other books? It's fine if you don't, but it's also true that part of these Lightning Literature courses is to explore this idea. What things might make a book literature? What keeps some books as just story books? Even if you can't exactly say what you think makes something literature, do you have some sense of certain books you think fall into each category?

13. Reb Itchele tells his son that the chance to study is like being offered pearls and gold coins, except that when one dies one cannot take money along. Do you feel like this about learning? Is it something precious to you? In what ways is it more valuable than money? Does our society place this same value on it? How can you tell?

14. Have you or a sibling held very different views about something from your parents? How do discussions about these things go? Are the participants able to talk pleasantly and rationally? Do the conversations get very emotional? If you are not one of the participants, with whom do you agree?

15. Singer says at one point he was overcome with the injustice of the world. Have you ever felt this way? In what circumstances? How have you learned to live with this feeling? Is there someone who represents to you the "ills of society" in the same way the cobbler does for Singer?

Workbook Answers

4.1.L EXAMINING YOUR CULTURE

Student answers will vary. There are no right or wrong answers here. If the student has trouble coming up with many, discuss possibilities together. Students may be somewhat blind to what is really part of their culture. For example, I currently live in a middle-class, white suburb and my answers would be:

Names:	Joe, Linda, John, Mark, Karen
Ways of Speaking:	"correct" grammar, non-accented, little slang
Occupations:	programmer, manager, teacher, real-estate agent—white collar, middle-class occupations
Foods:	barbeques in summer, organic produce
Holidays:	4th of July there are always fireworks in the neighborhood, people decorate a lot for Christmas
Values:	well-kept homes (people frequently do yard-work, there is a neighborhood association that enforces certain rules), comfort (people mostly drive huge vehicles without any practical need, spend a lot of money on material possessions), conformity (homes, vehicles, clothing are indistinguishable among most inhabitants).

4.2.L EXAMINING ANOTHER CULTURE

Some students will do better on this one than the last because they will be able to see another culture more clearly than their own. Other students will have more trouble, particularly if it involves research or involves investigating a culture near them that makes them uncomfortable. Obviously, the student should not be placed in a dangerous or even deeply uncomfortable situation. This may be something that the family can do together (for example, a visit to Chinatown together). If a family member, such as a grandparent, was raised in a different culture, the student could interview them.

4.3.M REWRITING FOR CLARITY (17 POINTS POSSIBLE)

1. Pronoun: she; nouns: Sarah, Rachel
2. Pronoun: their; nouns: Hasidic Jews, Reform Jews, Conservative Jews
3. Pronoun: it; nouns: matzoh balls; plain chicken soup.
4. Pronoun: he; nouns: Moshe, Ezekiel
5. Pronoun: he; nouns: Isaac Peretz, Mendele Mocher Sforim, and Sholem Aleichem

4.4.M REWRITING FOR WORDINESS (10 POINTS POSSIBLE)

1. The old man ate the gefilte fish.
2. The cantor sang the prayers.
3. Benjamin's sister playfully tugged his earlocks.
4. Rabbi Abraham taught Hebrew.
5. Daniel read the book of Esther for Purim this year.
6. Sarah baked the Challah loaf.
7. Max gave me that menorah.
8. My daughter, Rebekah, drew that beautiful Jewish star.
9. Many students took Judah's history of Israel class.
10. Chaim Topol played the part of Tevye in *Fiddler on the Roof.*

4.5.T A BRIEF INTRODUCTION TO YIDDISH (11 POINTS POSSIBLE)

1. Many Yiddish words have become part of English, giving a lovely spiciness to our language.
2. For example, someone is a *mensch* if they are a great guy, a *nudnik* if they are a pest, and a *schmuck* if they are even worse than a nudnik. To congratulate someone say, "*Mazl-tov!*", and rather than just complaining

you can *kvetch*; but if you take it too far they'll say you're a *meshuginah* ("crazy person").

3. The author's purpose is to inform.

4. Yiddish has invaded and infected English, dropping in words like dead birds falling out the trees.

5. Instead of meddling, now people *kibitz*; you don't do a good deed, you do a *mitzvah*; and instead of snacking, you *nosh*. I would rather drag something than *schlep* it; and if you're an unlucky person, do you really want to be called a *schlemazel*?

6. This author's primary purpose is to persuade.

7. These paragraphs both give the same basic information—that Yiddish words have become a part of the English language. They both show a bias on the writer's part. They both provide examples to support their point.

8. These paragraphs reveal opposite biases—the first writer is biased in favor of Yiddish, and the second is biased against Yiddish. The paragraphs give different examples. The first paragraph is more informative, while the second is more interested in persuading.

4.6.G CHOOSING THE RIGHT WORD (25 POINTS POSSIBLE)

Paragraph 1: number, it's, sense, there, to

Paragraph 2: Its, capital, you're, peace, sit, peak, sight

Paragraph 3: two, too, than, since

Paragraph 4: way, its, their, died, number

Paragraph 5: read, choose, way, past

4.7.A ANALYZING LITERATURE (14 OR 15 POINTS POSSIBLE)

1. The first indication that setting is important to this book is the book's title.

2. This passage is set in a village on the west bank of the Mississippi. (The student could be even more precise and say that the town is located somewhere between St. Louis and Keokuk.)

3. You could research Twain's childhood to see where he lived.

4. Answers will vary, but should be something pre-twentieth century as it is apparent there are no cars in this town.

5. You could research Twain's life to see when he was born; this will help narrow down the scene to within ten years or so.

6. The first mood of this passage could be described as sleepy, dull, or listless. The second mood is one of excitement.

7. The steamboat acts as a character by bringing excitement to the town, by changing the mood of the piece. In this way, it has an active role and this makes it more like a character.

8. Student must name three of the following: (1) the peaceful lapping of wavelets; (2) a negro drayman, famous for his quick eye and prodigious voice, lifts up the cry, "S-t-e-a-m-boat a-comin'!"; (3) a furious clatter of drays; (4) the pent steam is screaming through the gauge-cocks; (5) a bell rings; (6) the wheels stop, then turn back, churning the water to foam; and (7) such a yelling and cursing as the mates facilitate it all with.

9. Student must name one of the following: (1) the fragrant town drunkard; great volumes of the blackest smoke are rolling and (2) tumbling out of the chimneys.

10. Student must answer at least one of the following: (1) Twain provides several examples of technical terms relating to steamboats and steamboat towns and (2) Twain provides one quote from a townsman.

11. c

12. Twain uses alliteration in this phrase. (If your student has not taken Lightning Lit 7 and you have not previously studied alliteration, you may drop this question.)

4.8.P *A Day of Pleasure* Crossword Puzzle

4.9.P *A Day of Pleasure* Word Search

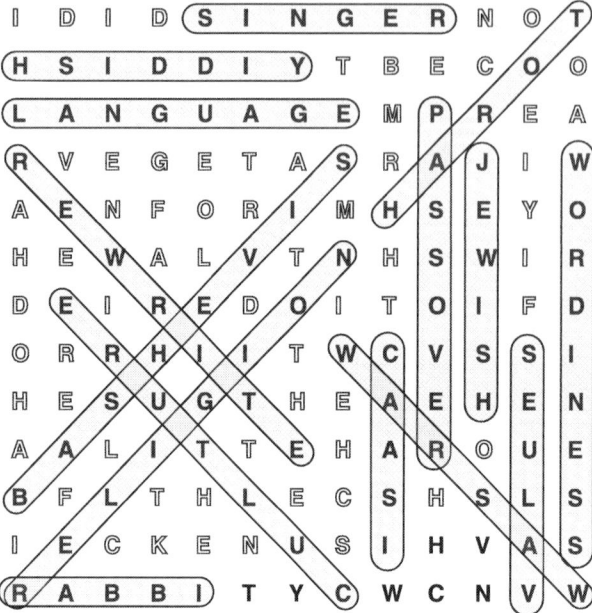

4.10.E The Nail

Answers will vary but the story should show aspects of culture and support the moral of "small things neglected can cause great trouble."

Chapter Five

"Wakefield" by Nathaniel Hawthorne

Stories and Poems for Extremely Intelligent Children of All Ages
   —Pages 254 to 261

Student Guide — Pages 89 to 111
Workbook — Pages 85 to 115

Chapter 5: "Wakefield"

Answers to Comprehension Questions

1. The narrator says he first read about Wakefield in a newspaper or magazine.

2. The story takes place in London.

3. Wakefield was apart from his wife for twenty years.

4. *Idea* is the antecedent of *it* and *Wakefield* is the antecedent of *his*.

5. c

6. Wakefield's wife realizes he enjoys keeping little secrets, so she indulges him and does not ask him about his journey.

7. No, Wakefield is not planning this when he leaves the house.

8. Wakefield smiles right before leaving the house.

9. Yes, Wakefield makes it to his new home unseen.

10. The narrator urges Wakefield to return to his wife.

11. Wakefield changes his mind because he wants to see how his wife and others will be affected by his absence. ("Vanity" is also an acceptable answer.)

12. Wakefield decides at first that he will wait for his wife to be frightened half-to-death before going back.

13. After Wakefield is gone for a number of weeks, his wife grows very ill.

14. After Wakefield's wife recovers, the narrator says that an impassable gulf has opened between the two of them.

15. b

16. d

17. Wakefield's situation is different from a hermit's because he still lives among people, even close to his wife, yet he does not have any contact with them.

18. The narrator leaves Wakefield as he is re-entering his former home.

Literary Lesson: Details in Writing

The student has already had some exposure to this idea through Chapter 3, "Vivid Imagery in Poetry." Students usually understand all the concepts I've presented here, but it often takes time for them to incorporate these concepts in all their writing. For example, a student may do a wonderful job on the writing exercise for this chapter, but then go on to write about an experience or write a persuasive paper for another lesson and completely forget to add important details. This is not unusual, so you shouldn't worry if it happens. Simply continue to remind students with any paper that details are important.

It can be good practice to read newspaper editorials and magazine articles together to see how well (or how poorly) the authors support their position with details. (Or, if the article is a story about something, to see how well details are used to tell the story.) I think it's excellent for students to always spend some time on current events, and this is best done with family discussing the event for some perspective. There is no reason, however, that along with discussing the social, political, religious, fiscal, etc., ramifications of events you cannot also discuss the writing style of the author. Indeed, how a writer approaches a piece can do a lot to determine how people view the event, so it is especially important to become a good critical reader of news. Whenever possible, choose three or more sources reporting on the same event. Compare and contrast how the writers use details. Do they choose different details to report on? Do they slant the same details in different ways? What can you tell about each author's purpose from the details each chose?

Mini-Lesson: Citing Information

The hardest part of citing information is just remembering the proper format, so expect students to use this mini-lesson (or a style guide) to help them for awhile. There's nothing wrong with this. If a student is in doubt about when to cite something, it's usually better to err on the side of citing it. As I say in the lesson, I strongly urge students to use the parenthetical method, as it is so much simpler than endnotes or footnotes.

Writing Exercises

In some ways the first exercise is the easiest because it allows the student to use some work already done in one of the workbook pages. The second exercise may be more appealing to some students, if they have an event they want to write about. The third exercise is the most creative, asking the student to do what Hawthorne did by writing a short story based on a news item. Students who enjoy short-story writing or who want to start will probably find this appealing. The fourth option is less creative, but would be good for students who need more practice with organization and support, if they are up to the challenge. The last exercise is the ubiquitous research paper. Again, the student may choose any topic for this.

Discussion Questions

1. Hawthorne says that individuals are all nicely adjusted to a system, and if we step out of that system we risk losing our place forever. What is your system? Who and what make it up? What is your place in that system? Have you ever stepped out of it? Have you ever thought about stepping out of it?

2. When a big change happens in life—going to college, getting married, the death of someone very close, etc.—how is that like having a change of system? How does changing a system in this way affect us? Why can it be so difficult? Can you think of any ways that might make it easier?

Workbook Answers

5.1.L EXAMINING DETAILS (7 POINTS POSSIBLE)

1. Student may list any three of the following: (1) gusty night, (2) frequent showers, (3) patter down, (4) a shower chances to fall, (5) driven by a gust into Wakefield's face and bosom, (6) he is quite penetrated with its autumnal chill, (7) wet and shivering.

2. Wakefield sees a fire.

3. Wakefield imagines that his wife will run to fetch his clothes for him.

4. Hawthorne tells us that Wakefield's legs are now stiffer, and so he ascends the steps to his house more heavily.

5. No, the narrator does not think Wakefield will be able to simply reenter his life. He says that Wakefield should not go inside, and the only home left to him is his grave.

5.2.L CHOOSING DETAILS FOR A PURPOSE

Student answers will vary. There should be several details for each purpose, and the details should vary (though there can be some overlap).

5.3.L ADDING DETAILS

Student answers will vary. Just be sure the appropriate type of detail has been added.

5.4.L RECOGNIZING SUPPORTING DETAILS (12 POINTS POSSIBLE)

1. The topic of this paragraph is that "Wakefield" demonstrates Nathaniel Hawthorne's interest in the alienation of people from society.

2. There are three details from the story given to support this point: (1) the main character alienates himself from society by leaving his wife but living near her for twenty years; (2) the assertion in the story that the character's life is even worse than that of a hermit; and (3) the physical description of the main character.

3. The topic of this paragraph is there are many reasons to rewrite a first draft.

4. The support the author gives is: (1) our first effort is not usually our best; (2) we can miss problems with grammar and mechanics on our first attempt; and (3) we need to remove excess words.

5. The topic of this paragraph is that citing sources is an important thing to do.

6. The support the author gives is: (1) citations make it easier for the reader to follow up on some aspect of your paper for more information; (2) citations allow the reader to check your original source to see if you're quoting out of context; and (3) it's important to give credit where credit is due.

5.5.M CITING SOURCES (10 POINTS POSSIBLE)

1. No
2. No
3. No
4. Yes
5. Yes
6. No
7. Yes
8. Yes
9. No
10. No

5.6.T EXAMINING AN ARGUMENT (12 POINTS POSSIBLE)

1. In the first sentence, the author claims the purpose of the pamphlet will be to inform.

2. The actual purpose of the pamphlet is to explain.

3. Most typically, an author will claim to be informing but actually be trying to persuade because they want to fool you into thinking their opinions are facts.

4. In the second sentence the author makes the assumption that everyone knows a vegetarian diet is healthier.

5. No, the author gives no source for this assertion.

6. Student answers may vary as to whether it is better, but the best answer to give is that it would be better to give the source. That allows the reader to check this source to be sure the author is not deceiving them. It also allows the reader to see how reliable the source is.

7. The author is assuming that the reader will find a big bowl of green beans more appetizing than a steak.

8. The author uses name-calling against meat-eaters by calling them animal-haters.

9. The only specific, factual statement the author makes is the third sentence: Consuming less meat means you will probably consume fewer fats, and that can help you lose weight.

10. Answers will vary; what is important is the student defends the answer well. I wrote this to be an especially weak argument, mostly devoid of facts, and dependent on poor assumptions, name calling, emotional ploys, etc. The hope is that most students will recognize this, at least in part. If a student does not, you may want to contrast these paragraphs with the instructions in the literary lesson for this chapter under "Details to Support an Idea" for writing a paper on a similar topic and supporting your assertions with facts.

5.7.G TYPES OF SENTENCES (10 POINTS POSSIBLE)

1. declarative sentence, simple sentence

2. declarative sentence, complex sentence

3. conditional sentence, compound sentence

4. That's a lot of green beans!

5. Either "Do you have a pet?" or "Would you want to see your dog or cat dragged off to a slaughter-house?"

6. imperative sentence, compound sentence

5.8.A ANALYZING LITERATURE

1. The first clue that setting is important to this story is that the setting is the title.

2. Student must list at least five of the following: (1) pewter dishes, (2) silver jugs, (3) tankards, (4) oak dresser, (5) oatcakes, (6) legs of beef, mutton, ham, (7) guns, (8) horse-pistols, (9) canisters, (10) green chairs, (11) black chairs, (12) a pointer dog, (13) puppies, (14) other dogs.

3. Student must list at least three of the following: (1) dark-skinned, (2) a gypsy, (3) a gentleman, (4) slovenly, (5) erect, (6) handsome, (7) morose.

4. The narrator shares that he has an aversion to showing displays of feeling. ("I bestow my own attributes over liberally on him.")

5. There are four: (1) the chatter of tongues; (2) the clatter of culinary utensils; (3) the squealing puppies; and (4) a long, guttural snarl.

6. The floor was of smooth, white stone.

7. From this, we can gather that Wuthering Heights and its inhabitants are not filled with life, in fact, they may be more dead than alive (the home does not nourish them).

5.9.P "WAKEFIELD" CROSSWORD PUZZLE

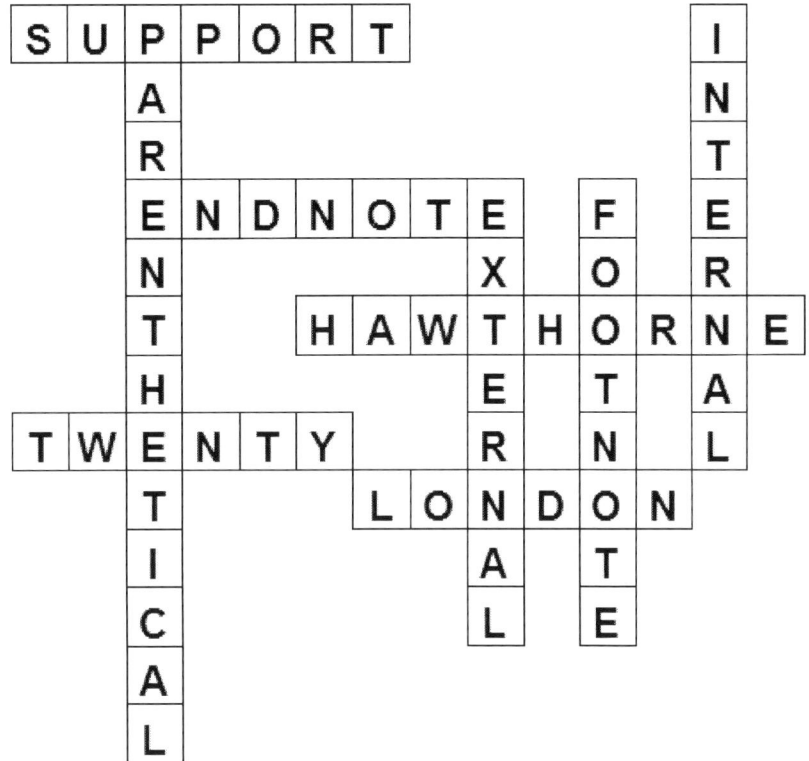

5.10.P "WAKEFIELD" WORD SEARCH

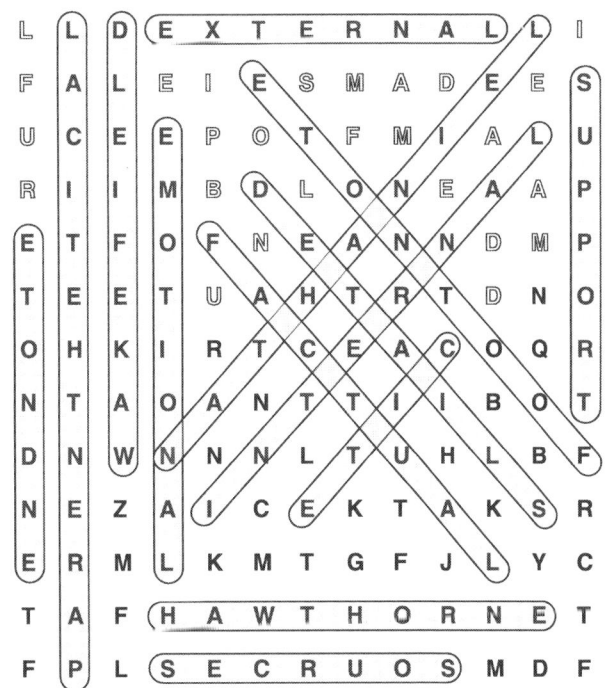

5.11.E ENDURANCE IN WRITING PARAGRAPHS (11 POINTS POSSIBLE)

1. 1

2. 3, 4, 5

3. (1) Frank Worsley was captain.

   (2) July, midwinter in Antarctica, long polar nights for weeks.

   (3) -30 degrees Fahrenheit, a sea of ice all around.

   (4) The wind shrieked.

   (5) Worsley and two others would hear the ice groan.

   (6) The ships timbers would quiver from the stress of the ice.

   (7) One man spoke.

   Answers will vary for rewriting the paragraph, but it should contain all of the above information, but in a very simple manner.

4. Sentence 7.

5. What he said.

   Answers will vary but the student's new paragraph about their own adventure should include a topic sentence, supporting detail, and a closing sentence that makes the reader want to continue. It should also contain vivid language and enough detail to make it enjoyable to the reader.

5.12.E A FIRE KINDLED (8 POINTS POSSIBLE)

1. Paragraph One

2. Paragraph Three

3. Paragraph Two

4. Paragraph Three

5. Paragraph One

6. Paragraph One

7. Answers will vary.

8. Answers will vary, but students should be able to support their answers.

Chapter Six

A Christmas Carol by Charles Dickens

Student Guide — Pages 113 to 134

Workbook — Pages 117 to 140

Chapter 6: *A Christmas Carol*

Answers to Comprehension Questions

CHAPTER 1: MARLEY'S GHOST

1. Scrooge and Marley were business partners.

2. Student answers will vary, but should be something along the lines of: Scrooge is greedy, envious, hard, secret, solitary, cold, bad-tempered, mean, thinks only of money, uncaring.

3. Other people avoided Scrooge whenever possible.

4. This story begins on Christmas eve.

5. Scrooge's nephew angers him by wishing him a merry Christmas.

6. Marley has been dead for seven years.

7. The two men want Scrooge to donate money to the poor.

8. Scrooge has an improved opinion of himself because he has turned down their request for money and successfully sent them on their way.

9. Scrooge says it is unfair that he has to pay his clerk's wages for a day when the clerk does no work.

10. Scrooge sees Marley's face in the knocker.

11. Scrooge likes darkness because it is cheap.

12. Marley's chain is made up of cashboxes, keys, padlocks, ledgers, deeds, and heavy purses. (The student need not name every item exactly, but just give the general idea.)

13. He says that his senses may cheat him, for example if he has eaten something bad.

14. Scrooge outwardly acts calm and skeptical and makes smart conversation; inside he is terrified.

15. The ghost removes the bandage from its head and its lower jaw drops down to its breast.

16. Marley has appeared before Scrooge to warn him about his fate and tell him he has a chance to escape it.

17. Three ghosts will visit Scrooge.

18. The misery afflicting all of them is that they want to help people but cannot.

CHAPTER 2: THE FIRST OF THE THREE SPIRITS

1. According to the clock it is midnight.

2. The Ghost of Christmas Past visits Scrooge.

3. The first place the ghost takes Scrooge is a country road in the place where Scrooge was born.

4. No, the people that Scrooge and the ghost see cannot see them.

5. The boy that Scrooge and the ghost see in the school is Scrooge, and he is reading.

6. These other people they see are characters from books.

7. Scrooge wishes he had given him something.

8. Scrooge's sister comes to see him to bring him home.

9. Scrooge's master's name is Fezziwig.

10. They have a Christmas party and dance in the warehouse.

11. Scrooge sees how happy his former master made him, and he now wishes he could do so for his clerk.

12. Scrooge is mostly like with his fiancée.

13. Scrooge has now become greedy and obsessed with money.

14. Scrooge is unable to hide the ghost's light.

CHAPTER 3: THE SECOND OF THE THREE SPIRITS

1. Scrooge is scared because no spirit appears but there is a light in his room.

2. Student must name two of the following: (1) the walls and ceiling are covered in holly, mistletoe, and ivy; (2) there's a huge fire in the fireplace; (3) there's a pile of turkeys, geese, game, poultry and other food on the floor; (4) there is a Giant sitting on top of this pile.

3. The second spirit is the Ghost of Christmas Present.

4. He means there have been more than eighteen hundred Christmases.

5. This ghost first takes Scrooge to the city streets on Christmas morning.

6. They go to Bob Cratchit's, Scrooge's clerk's, house.

7. Tiny Tim hoped the people saw him in the church because he is a cripple and he wants them to "remember upon Christmas Day, who made lame beggars walk and blind men see." (Students need not quite exactly; they can just give the gist of this.)

8. Bob Cratchit says this about their pudding.

9. Scrooge asks the ghost if Tiny Tim will live. The ghost says if the future is not altered, Tiny Tim will die.

10. The ghost uses Scrooge's phrase, "decrease the surplus population."

11. Bob Cratchit proposes a toast to Scrooge.

12. Student must name one of the following: to a (1) miner's home on the moors, (2) lighthouse, and (3) ship at sea.

13. The spirit then takes Scrooge to his nephew's house.

14. Dickens says the most contagious thing in the world is laughter and good-humour.

15. He means that Scrooge acts in a way that hurts himself, for example, by not spending money on himself and others and by not having friends to enjoy life with.

16. Scrooge begs the spirit to let him stay until all the guests have left.

17. As the night goes on, the ghost looks older.

18. The ghost brings two children from his robes to show to Scrooge, Ignorance and Want.

19. The ghost says, "Are there no prisons? Are there no workhouses?"

CHAPTER 4: THE LAST OF THE SPIRITS

1. The only part of this last ghost that can be seen is a hand.

2. The ghost says nothing to him.

3. Scrooge guesses this is the Ghost of Christmas Yet To Come.

4. This spirit first has Scrooge listen to some businessmen talking.

5. This talk puzzles Scrooge because they are talking about someone having died, but he doesn't know who it could be.

6. The spirit takes Scrooge to a shop in a poor part of town.

7. People who have stolen Scrooge's things have brought them there to sell.

8. Student must name one of the following: (1) the bed-curtains, (2) the blankets, (3) the shirt Scrooge was to be buried in.

9. The spirit next takes him to the room of the dead man. He wants Scrooge to draw back the sheet and look at the dead man's face, but Scrooge cannot.

10. The spirit takes Scrooge to a graveyard.

11. Scrooge asks the spirit if these are shadows of things that Will be or shadows of things that May be. The spirit does not answer, only continues to point.

CHAPTER 5: THE END OF IT

1. Scrooge says he will live in the Past, Present, and Future.

2. Scrooge tells the boy to buy the big prize turkey. He sends it to Bob Cratchit's.

3. Scrooge says this because that is where he first saw Marley's Ghost's face.

4. Scrooge goes to his nephew's house.

5. Scrooge pretends to be angry that Bob is late. But he then gives Bob a raise, which makes Bob think for a moment that Scrooge has gone insane.

Literary Lesson: Character

Anything approaching a thorough understanding of character in literature is very complex; this lesson only touches the surface. I chose *A Christmas Carol* for this lesson in part because Scrooge is such an extreme character who goes through such a dramatic transformation; my hope is that this will help students see these things more clearly. If your student feels uncertain about any aspect, discuss how Jim is developed in *Treasure Island*. Also, when the student gets to Chapter 8 (*The Hobbit*), discuss how Bilbo is developed, as this book is another excellent example of character development. Short stories are generally not as good a venue for this topic. One good exception to this in *Stories and Poems* is "Rikki-Tikki-Tavi" which students who have used the Lightning Lit Guide Grade 7 will have already read. You can discuss how Rikki is developed, what changes his character goes through, and what brings about those changes. (If your student has not read this story, it may be good for them to do so, as it doesn't take long and is good for a discussion of character.)

Mini-Lesson: The Narrator

Narrators are quite varied in literature, and it's mostly important that the student understand that stories have narrators and that the narrator is not the same as the author. This is a common mistake students make. (Of course, in the case of nonfiction, like *A Day of Pleasure*, the narrator is the author.) The mini-lesson discusses the narrators of most of the readings in this class so far, but you can also discuss the narrator of "Wakefield" since I do not cover that story in this mini-lesson. This narrator is similar to the narrator of *A Christmas Carol*. He is not a character in the story in the same way Jim is in *Treasure Island*, but he is a narrator with personality. Read the story together and pick out those passages that show us the personality of this narrator. Ask the student to describe this narrator as best as they can.

Writing Exercises

The first exercise will be the easiest for most students because it allows them to use work they've already done in the workbook pages. The second one will require more work from the student, but will probably be more appealing to students who prefer to write nonfiction. The third addresses the mini-lesson rather than the lesson and requires a certain amount of analysis on the student's part though it is expressed in a creative way. The fourth addresses both the lesson and mini-lesson. Finally, we again have a research paper. As usual, students should follow all directions given so far for a research paper.

Discussion Questions

1. On page 7, Scrooge's nephew gives a beautiful speech about Christmas. Discuss this speech. What do you think of his ideas of Christmas? What are your ideas of Christmas? Do you disagree with Scrooge's nephew in any way? Is there anything you would add?

2. Marley's ghost tells Scrooge, "It is required of every man. . . that the spirit within him should walk abroad among his fellow-men, and travel far and wide. . ." (23) Do you believe this is required of all of us during life? What does walking abroad with your fellow man mean to you? Do you think this is something you do?

3. Marley and the ghosts that Scrooge sees when he looks out his window are bound by chains that they forged from the way they conducted their lives. For example, Marley was interested only in his business, so he is chained by items of his business. Is there anything in your life that could possibly become your chain, that is, that could become more important to you than it should be and keep you from the truly important "business" of life? What things would be part of this chain? Even if there's nothing now, can you imagine that this might happen when you get older, say, as you go to college or start life on your own? What ways can you think of to avoid forging this sort of chain, to keep your priorities straight? Does visualizing this problem as a chain, rather than an abstract concept, help you in any way?

4. What do you think the Ghost of Christmas Past would show you? That is, what events from your life so far have helped make you the person you are today? Does thinking about these events sometimes soften your heart, in the way Scrooge's heart was softened by seeing his past life?

5. Between his apprenticeship with Fezziwig and the breaking of his engagement, something happened to change Scrooge, though we are not shown any one event that causes this change. Do you feel there has been a time in your life when you underwent a significant change? Was it for

the better or for the worse? How would you describe yourself both before and afterward?

6. The Ghost of Christmas Present is a symbol for how Christmas touches (or should touch) everyone's heart. When the ghost is near these people or sprinkles his magic, they are more joyful and more kind. Does Christmas have this effect on you and other people you know? If it has this effect on some people you know but not others, why do you think this is? Why are some people cheered by Christmas, while others are not affected, and still others are even depressed by it? What things can help other people to be cheered by Christmas?

7. Would you want to see your future, as Scrooge does? If it were a future that you could change by changing your present course of action (as opposed to a future that was set in stone), would that make a difference?

8. Scrooge is impacted by seeing the past, present, and future. Which do you think would impact you the most, if you could be shown these things as Scrooge was? Why?

9. Since we can't be visited by spirits like these, in what ways can we use the past, present and future to help us become better people?

10. Several Christmas traditions are mentioned in this story. What Christmas traditions do you have? Can you think of any others you would like to adopt or start?

Workbook Answers

6.1.L CREATING A CHARACTER

Answers will vary. Do not score this page; it's just a place for the student to get started.

6.2.L DESCRIPTION

Answers will vary. This should be a single descriptive paragraph. Be sure the student has only addressed one or two aspects of the character rather than trying to give a complete biography of someone.

6.3.L OPINIONS OF OTHERS

Answers will vary. This should be in dialogue form. (Students who have taken the Grade-7 Lightning Literature course should know how to properly format and punctuate dialogue, so feel free to grade on this point as well.) The dialogue should be between two characters discussing the character your student created in 6.1.L. It should be clear how these two characters feel about this character.

6.4.L BACK STORY

Answers will vary. This just needs to be a back story in any form the student chooses.

6.5.L ACTIONS

Answers will vary. This just needs to show something about the character through their actions.

6.6.L SPEECH

Answers will vary. This just needs to show something about the character through their speech.

6.7.L CHANGE

Answers will vary.

6.8.A ANALYZING LITERATURE (10 POINTS POSSIBLE)

1. Jane Austen uses description in her opening paragraph.

2. Jane Austen uses back story in her second paragraph.

3. In the first dialogue, Jane Austen uses the character's speech, the opinion of others (Emma's father), and actions.

4. In the second dialogue, Jane Austen uses the character's speech, the opinion of others, and actions.

5. The third paragraph demonstrates foreshadowing. (The last paragraph is also a possible answer, though the third paragraph is a better one.) (If your student has not taken Lightning Lit 7 and you have not previously studied foreshadowing, you may drop this question.)

6. The setting for this story is evidently a large home, some time before the inventions of cars. We know it is large because Emma's father says their home is three times as large as the Randalls'; also it is pointed out that the Woodhouses are rich. This is almost certainly before cars because they talk of taking a carriage, and a rich family would almost certainly own a car if one were available. An extremely well-informed and observant student might also note that this passage contains British spellings of words and deduce that this story takes place in England, but that would be extra credit. (If the student knows that Jane Austen was an English writer and/or knows when she lived, that is also fair information to use here; but I would still want such students to take clues from the text as well.)

6.9.P *A CHRISTMAS CAROL* CROSSWORD PUZZLE

6.10.P *A CHRISTMAS CAROL* WORD SEARCH

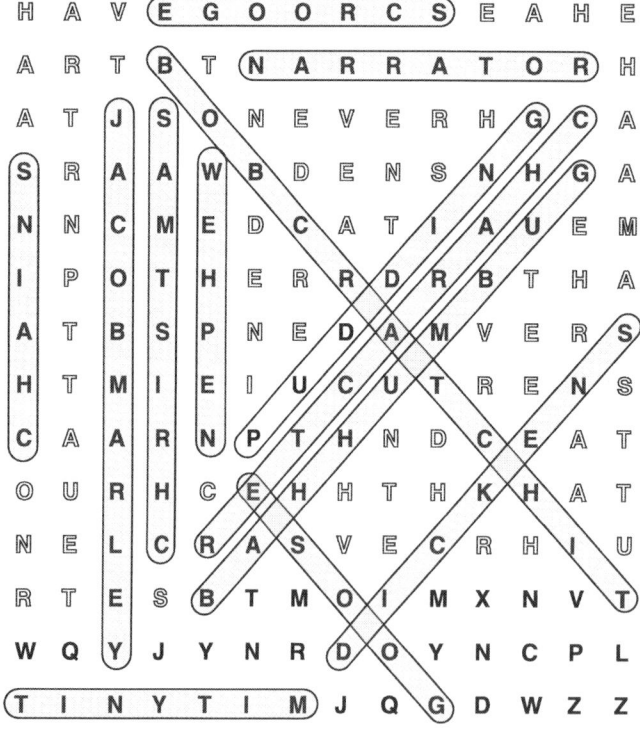

6.11.E TONE AND MOOD

Answers may vary, but your student should be able to support the terms chosen. Terms listed would be our recommendations. It's also fine for students to chose other words of their own to describe the piece.

1. This is an unusual paragraph that would fit different tones including formal, serious, optimistic, and pessimistic

2. Formal, serious, sad

3. Formal, serious, sad, sorrowful

4. Informal, humorous, sad

5. Informal, serious, humorous, sorrowful

6. Formal, serious, imaginary, pessimistic

Chapter Seven

Figurative Language

Stories and Poems for Extremely Intelligent Children of All Ages

Chapter 7: Figurative Language

Answers to Comprehension Questions

"GOBLIN MARKET"
1. The goblins are selling fruit.
2. Laura looks at the goblins, but Lizzie does not.
3. The goblins repeat "Come buy."
4. The goblins request a lock of her hair for payment.
5. Yes, Laura enjoys the fruit very much.
6. Jeanie pined away for the goblins and their gifts until she died.
7. Laura tells Lizzie she will buy more fruit and bring some to Lizzie.
8. No, Laura never hears the goblins' cry again.
9. Lizzie goes to the goblins because she fears Laura is dying.
10. The goblins want Lizzie to eat with them.
11. When Laura tastes the juice of the goblins' fruit on Lizzie, who had refused to eat the fruit, the spell is broken.

"A LEAVE-TAKING"
1. d

"AUTUMN"
There are no comprehension questions for this poem.

"WEEP YOU NO MORE, SAD FOUNTAINS"
1. The "sad fountains" are eyes.

"LOVE WILL FIND OUT THE WAY"
There are no comprehension questions for this poem.

"WHO HAS SEEN THE WIND?"
Student must name one of the following: (1) the leaves hang trembling, (2) the trees bow down their heads.

"THE SILVER SWAN"

There are no comprehension questions for this poem.

"THE SNOWSTORM"

There are no comprehension questions for this poem.

Literary Lesson: Figurative Language

Students usually have no difficulty understanding these concepts. The most common difficulty comes with metaphors. I know of no better way to solidify understanding of figurative language than simply looking for it while reading. If the student feels unsure about the nature of an allegory, don't worry too much about that yet. One allegory many students have already read, however, is *The Chronicles of Narnia*. If your student has read one or more of the books in this series, discuss how they are allegories for various biblical stories. Perhaps the easiest one to discuss in this manner is *The Lion, The Witch and The Wardrobe*. Another book some students will have read that is an even more obvious allegory is *The Pilgrims Progress*. If your student is really struggling with the idea of allegory, take some time to read part of this book together. Explain that each character is representative of something else. (It will be easy to see this since the characters are named for what they represent.) Reading this entire book would also be good for an advanced student who wants more of a challenge with this class.

NOTE: If your student still has trouble understanding poetry that has no rhyme or meter (such as free verse, covered in the mini-lesson in Chapter 3), review this lesson, Chapter 3 of this book, and Chapter 7 of the Grade-7 Lightning Lit guide (if you own this book). These are elements of poetry besides rhyme and meter. Next, find some poetry without obvious rhyme or meter and look for these elements in the poems. This can help the student appreciate poetic elements besides the more obvious rhyme and meter.

Mini-Lesson: Fun Poems

Students should have no trouble getting the gist of these poem types. If a student wants more challenge, you can introduce some of these variations:

- In a double-acrostic, the first *and* last letters of each line read down to spell words or phrases.
- An acrostic can be written wherein the first letter of the first line, second letter of the second line, third letter of the third line, etc. spell the word or phrase.

■ The student can write a cento that only uses lines from one poet's poems or from poems of a particular time period.

Writing Exercises

Students who do not like to write poetry will probably find it easiest to do the first exercise as a prose exercise. The poetry exercises are equal in difficulty; it just depends on what subject matter or type of poetry the student is interested in. The fourth and sixth exercises are also prose possibilities (the fourth can be poetry or prose). The sixth also addresses using details for supporting an argument.

Discussion Questions

1. "Goblin Market" tells a story, as have some other poems you've read this year. Do you prefer poems that tell a story or poems that describe a scene or a feeling?

2. How effective do you think "Goblin Market" is as an allegory of temptation, sin, and redemption? Do you think, if you had not known that's what it was, that you would have spotted the allegorical meaning? Do you think most people would? Now that you know what it is, do you think any of the images will help you in any way in your life?

3. Lizzie and Laura are very close, before and after Laura's transgression. Are you this close to anyone? Do you feel you could do for someone what Lizzie did for Laura, or do you know anyone who would do so for you?

4. "Weep You No More, Sad Fountains" is about the loss of a loved one. If you have endured such a loss, is there anything in this poem that you can relate to? Is there anything in this poem that you think might comfort someone who has lost a loved one?

5. "A Leave-Taking" and "Love Will Find Out the Way" are both poems about love, but they have very different points of view. Although they are about romantic love, most of the sentiments in them would also be true about love between friends or family. Have you experienced love in either way that is expressed in these two poems? For example, have you had a good friend who suddenly was not your friend any more who "would not hear" and "would not love"? Or, have you had a family member who went to such great lengths for you, that is was apparent that their love would "find out the way"? If you have not personally had these experiences, have you seen either type of love in other people? What parts of these poems seem to portray these types of love particularly well?

Workbook Answers

7.1.L IDENTIFYING FIGURES OF SPEECH (10 POINTS POSSIBLE)

1. personification
2. personification
3. simile
4. simile
5. simile
6. personification
7. metaphor
8. metaphor
9. metaphor
10. personification

7.2.L CREATING SIMILES (10 POINTS POSSIBLE)

Student answers will vary. Be sure each is a simile. After discussing any that seem less than creative (tired or a cliché), see if your student can come up with a better answer.

7.3.L CREATING METAPHORS (10 POINTS POSSIBLE)

Student answers will vary. Be sure each is a metaphor. After discussing any that seem less than creative (tired or a cliché), see if your student can come up with a better answer.

7.4.L CREATING PERSONIFICATION (10 POINTS POSSIBLE)

Student answers will vary. Be sure each is a personification. After discussing any that seem less than creative (tired or a cliché), see if your student can come up with a better answer.

7.5.L CREATING AN ALLEGORY (9 POINTS POSSIBLE)

Answers will vary. If you don't understand one or more of the student's answers, ask for an explanation.

7.6.M WRITING AN ACROSTIC

Answers will vary. The only requirement is it be an acrostic of the student's name.

7.7.A ANALYZING LITERATURE (7, 8, OR 9 POINTS POSSIBLE)

1. Dickinson uses a simile then personification.

2. Dickinson uses a metaphor.

3. No, she is not using a figure of speech. She is simply making a comparison between the bodice and the vest, but she is not using a simile because these two items are very similar. In fact, she is emphasizing the similarity between the two, because the bodice and vest are representative of the man and woman. (Students need only give the information in the first two sentences here to be given full credit. The third sentence is just some additional information.)

4. Dickinson is describing love (or the act of a man and woman falling in love or being in love).

5. The two people have fallen in love and gotten together.

6. Dickinson uses alliteration in this line. (If your student has not taken Lightning Lit 7 and you have not previously studied alliteration, you may drop this question.)

7. Dickinson uses assonance in this line. (If your student has not taken Lightning Lit 7 and you have not previously studied assonance, you may drop this question.)

7.8.P FIGURATIVE LANGUAGE CROSSWORD PUZZLE

7.9.P FIGURATIVE LANGUAGE WORD SEARCH

7.10.E POETRY FOR YOUR BIRTHDAY (11 POINTS POSSIBLE)

1. none
2. three
3. singing bird, apple tree, rainbow shell
4. calm or peaceful
5. a couch
6. merry, helpful, happy and answers will vary but should express happy or lighthearted

7.11.E TOOLS OF THE TRADE (8 POINTS POSSIBLE)

1. simile
2. irony
3. personification
4. oxymoron
5. hyperbole
6. paradox
7. none of these
8. metaphor

Answers will vary for the rest of this assignment.

Chapter Eight

The Hobbit by J.R.R. Tolkien

Student Guide—Pages 153 to 176

Workbook—Pages 163 to 185

Chapter 8: *The Hobbit*

Answers to Comprehension Questions

CHAPTER I

1. Student must name one of the following: (1) They are rich, (2) they never have any adventures, and (3) they never do anything unexpected.

2. The Tooks were not as respectable as the Bagginses because they were not entirely hobbit-like and would sometimes go and have adventures.

3. Bilbo decides that Gandalf is not his sort because Gandalf is looking for someone to go on an adventure.

4. Gandalf puts a secret mark on Bilbo's door, then removes it the next day by banging on it with his staff.

5. Thorin is the most important of the dwarves.

6. Gandalf's sign on Bilbo's door brought the dwarves there.

7. The dwarves doubt Bilbo's suitability for this journey because he shrieks in terror during Thorin's speech.

8. Dragons pile up the gold they steal, then sleep on it.

CHAPTER II

1. Bilbo feels both relief and disappointment when he thinks the others have left without him.

2. Gandalf disappears suddenly.

3. Bilbo tries to pick one of the trolls' pockets.

4. The trolls want to cook and eat Bilbo and the dwarves.

5. When the sun comes up, the trolls are turned to stone.

CHAPTER III

1. Bilbo loves elves but is also a bit afraid of them. Dwarves don't like elves; they think they are foolish.

2. There is little to tell because it is such a good stay.

3. Student must name at least two of the following: (1) the travelers are refreshed from their rest in his home; (2) their clothes are mended; their bruises heal; (3) they gain renewed hope; (4) they get clothes and provisions; (5) Elrond gives them advice; (6) Elrond interprets the runes on the swords, thus identifying them; and (7) Elrond discovers and reads moon letters on the map.

CHAPTER IV

1. The party enters the cave to escape the storm and the giants throwing rocks.

2. Gandalf is not captured by the goblins.

3. The goblins particularly hate Thorin's people because those dwarves fought in the Goblin-wars.

4. Thorin's sword (which killed many goblins in the war) enrages the goblins.

CHAPTER V

1. When goblins are around, an elvish sword or dagger glows.

2. Gollum lives in the lake.

3. Bilbo and Gollum have a riddle competition. If Bilbo wins, Gollum will show him the way out; if Gollum wins, he gets to eat Bilbo.

4. No, Gollum once lived with his grandmother in a hole in a bank by a river.

5. Bilbo wins by asking Gollum, "What have I got in my pocket?" This isn't quite fair because it's not a proper riddle.

6. Gollum goes to the island to get his gold ring. He wants it to become invisible and attack Bilbo.

7. Gollum attacks Bilbo because he realizes that Bilbo has his ring.

8. Bilbo escapes the goblins by putting on his ring and becoming invisible.

CHAPTER VI

1. Bilbo is able to sneak up on the party by using the ring to be invisible. No, he does not yet reveal this to the others.

2. The party must get on the road right away because the goblins will be after them.

3. Bilbo says, "Escaping goblins to be caught by wolves!"

4. The Wargs are at the clearing to meet the goblins to help them with a raid.

5. Gandalf lights pine cones on fire and throws them among the Wargs, burning them. This attracts the attention of the Lord of the Eagles.

6. The eagles will not take the party to where men live, because the men would shoot at them with arrows.

CHAPTER VII

1. Beorn allows the gathering party to stay because he is so interested in Gandalf's story.

2. While the party slept, a meeting of bears has apparently taken place outside.

3. Beorn speaks with the Warg and the goblin to verify Gandalf's story.

4. Beorn warns them especially not to stray from the path in Mirkwood.

5. Student must name one of the following: Beorn follows the party on their journey to Mirkwood to (1) guard them, (2) guide them, and (3) keep an eye on his ponies.

6. Student must name one of the following: (1) Bilbo and the dwarves are dismayed because they have to send their ponies back, (2) they have heavy packs to carry, (3) Gandalf is leaving them, and (4) they have to go through Mirkwood.

CHAPTER VIII

1. At night the only things they could see were eyes.

2. The party crosses the enchanted stream by using a boat which they find on the other side. Bombur almost drowns, but instead is enchanted by the water and falls into a deep sleep.

3. The dwarves waste their arrows by shooting at deer.

4. They leave the path because they see a light and are hoping to find food.

5. Bilbo feels fiercer and bolder after killing the giant spider who had attacked him.

6. Bilbo names his dagger Sting.

7. Bilbo sings to the spiders to anger them and draw them away from the dwarves. Also, he wants the dwarves to hear him and know he is trying to help.

8. Bilbo tells the dwarves about his ring because he sees no other way to escape the spiders.

9. Thorin becomes separated from the others. He is taken by the Wood-elves.

CHAPTER IX

1. When the Wood-elves appear, Bilbo puts on his ring then follows the elves and dwarves.

2. Bilbo returns the keys to the guard because the guard was kind to the prisoners and Bilbo hopes to save him some trouble with the king. Also, he thinks it will make their disappearance seem more magical.

3. Bilbo himself is not in a barrel. He clings onto a barrel and floats out with them that way.

CHAPTER X

1. The people of Lake-town are impressed by Thorin because they still tell legends of his father and grandfather. They are confident that Thorin will defeat the dragon and bring riches back from the mountain.

2. The Master of the town isn't sure Thorin is really a descendent of the kings.

CHAPTER XI

1. Student must name at least one of the following which Bilbo and the dwarves see: (1) the ruins of the town, (2) the dark cavernous opening, steam and (3) dark smoke, dark crows.

2. Their hopes are raised when they discover the path and the door, but they are dashed again when they can't get through the door.

3. Bilbo finally figures out how to open the door.

CHAPTER XII

1. Student must name at least one of the following: (1) the tunnel begins to get warmer, (2) Bilbo sees a red glow ahead, (3) wisps of vapour float past Bilbo, and (4) he hears the dragon snoring.

2. During his first encounter with the dragon, Bilbo steals a two-handled cup.

3. They can't immediately rush inside because they must save Bofur and Bombur.

4. Bilbo replies to Smaug with riddles.

5. While Smaug talks to Bilbo, Bilbo begins to doubt his friends and also feels an urge to tell the whole truth to the dragon.

6. Bilbo wants Smaug to roll over so he can find a weak spot in his armor.

7. The party enters the mountain and shuts the door because they know Smaug will now be able to find it.

8. Smaug is particularly puzzled because he has never smelled anything like Bilbo before.

CHAPTER XIII

1. Bilbo is frightened when a bat brushes against him and he drops his torch which goes out.

2. The sight of gold and jewels make a dwarf bold.

3. They see a gathering of many birds.

CHAPTER XIV

1. Bard hears about the weak spot in Smaug's armor from the thrush who heard Bilbo talking about it.

2. After Smaug is dead, the people want Bard as their king rather than the Master because Bard killed Smaug while the Master only tried to escape. The Master diverts their attention to the dwarves by blaming them for sending the dragon to the town in the first place.

3. The people are cheered by the thought of all the unguarded gold on the mountain.

CHAPTER XV

1. A raven, Roac, tells Bilbo and the dwarves that Smaug is dead.

2. Roac also tells them that the men of Lake-town and the Wood-elves know about Smaug's death and are intent on having the treasure for themselves.

3. Student must name one of the following: (1) Bard killed Smaug, (2) Bard is the descendent of Girion of Dale and much of his wealth is in the dragon's lair, (3) Smaug caused much damage to the Lake-town whose people had helped Thorin.

4. Thorin tells Bard to get rid of the elves and to put down his weapons.

CHAPTER XVI

1. Bilbo gives the Arkenstone to Bard to help Bard in his bargaining with Thorin because Bilbo wants the adventure to end and to be able to go home.

2. Bard, the Elvinking, and Gandalf all admire Bilbo for bringing the Arkenstone to Bard.

CHAPTER XVII

1. Thorin is furious and threatens to throw Bilbo onto the rocks.

2. Thorin agrees to give Bard and the Elvenking one fourteenth of the treasure (Bilbo's share) for the Arkenstone. He is hoping that his cousin, Dain, will arrive in time to fight for it.

3. The dwarves attack first.

4. The attack is interrupted by a swarm of bats (and by Gandalf) which heralds the coming of goblins.

5. The five armies are the Goblins, the Wild Wolves (Wargs), the Elves, the Men, and the Dwarves.

6. The Eagles come to help. (If the student is answering this after having already read chapter XVIII, Beorn is also an acceptable answer.)

7. We know he lives because we've already read that he was very fond later of telling about this battle.

CHAPTER XVIII

1. Bilbo was not found for a long time because he had his ring on and was invisible.

2. Thorin, Fili, and Kili die in the battle.

3. Thorin is buried with the Arkenstone on his chest and his sword, Orcrist, on his tomb.

CHAPTER XIX

1. The adventure has taken a year.

2. Bilbo finds that his relatives are auctioning off his things.

3. Most other hobbits now find Bilbo unrespectable. Bilbo does not care about this though.

Literary Lesson: Conflict

Conflict is a pretty easy concept for most students to grasp. If a student has trouble, review *A Christmas Carol* together. The conflicts in this book are fairly obvious, and it can help reinforce these ideas.

Mini-Lesson: Genre Fiction

The concept here is a simple one. If you need to, an easy way to look at the different genres is simply to visit a bookstore together. Usually, fiction is categorized in a bookstore by its genre. If your student is interested in exploring a certain genre, here are some authors I can recommend both for their writing skill and for their appropriateness for junior-high students:

MYSTERY:

Agatha Christie, Rex Stout, Sir Arthur Conan Doyle, G.K. Chesterton (Father Brown)

FANTASY:

George MacDonald (though he can be a bit heavy going), J. R. R. Tolkien, C. S. Lewis (not everything by these writers is fantasy)

SCIENCE FICTION:

Isaac Asimov, Ray Bradbury (not everything by these authors is science fiction), Stanislov Lem (he can be heavy going as well), Douglas Adams (for humorous science fiction)

WESTERN:

Zane Grey, Louis L'Amour (note that I have not actually read either of these authors, but my understanding is they are appropriate for junior high students)

ADVENTURE:

Robert Louis Stephenson, H. Rider Haggard (these may contain some material that some parents will find inappropriate), Patrick O'Brian, C. S. Forester, (these two are authors of sea adventures), G. A. Henty

HORROR:

Edgar Allan Poe (though I think horror stories are often a bad idea for students before high-school)

ROMANCE:

Madeleine L'Engle has written some, including *A Ring of Endless Light*, *The Arm of the Starfish*, *Camilla*, and *Troubling a Star*. Also, some of the novels of George MacDonald which include romances that would be appropriate for the advanced reader, have been paraphrased by Michael Phillips, such as *The Fisherman's Lady*.

Writing Exercises

None of these is really any easier than the others. Students who like to write about themselves and their lives will prefer the first one. The second one combines creativity with analysis. The third is for the student who loves to write stories. The last is the research option. I chose topics that relate to Tolkien, but the unmotivated student should be allowed to choose any topic. Be sure all parts so far covered about writing a research paper are properly done in the paper.

Discussion Questions

1. Bilbo obviously loves his home very much, and it is a great comfort to him. How do you feel about your home? What things make it comfortable for you? What things make it unique and homey? Is there anything you would like to change to make it more so?

2. Bilbo's hobbit society says that adventuring is not respectable. Do you do things or have beliefs that are looked down on by your society? What are they? How does that make you feel? Tolkien says that when Bilbo returned from his adventure he didn't care that his society disapproved of him. Why do you think that was? Are there things you can do to help you care less about what society thinks of you? Or do you think it's important to fit into your society and be accepted by them?

3. Bilbo misses his home greatly when he's on his adventure and thinks of it often. Have you ever had to spend a long time away from home? How did it feel? Did you think of it often? What did you do, or what could you do, to make home feel nearer when you're away from it?

4. Bilbo often doubts that he chose correctly in going on this adventure. Have you ever done something—something that took awhile to finish— that you began to have doubts about? What was it, and what caused your doubts? Did anything eventually ease those doubts or did they prove to be justified? What sorts of things cause people to have doubts about what they're doing?

5. Bilbo also doubted himself at times when the dwarves were depending on him, for example, when he was the only one able to get them away from the Wood-elves. Have there been times when people depended on you and you were unsure of yourself? How did that feel? Were you able to come through for them?

6. Tolkien says that Bilbo "fought the real battle in the tunnel alone" when he decided to approach Smaug. Tolkien calls this the "bravest thing" Bilbo did. Has there been a time when you had to make a hard decision, perhaps overcome a fear, on your own? How did that feel? Did you make the right decision? Did it feel brave? Even if you didn't make the right decision previously, do you think picturing Bilbo fighting "the real battle in the tunnel alone" might help you make better choices in the future?

7. Bilbo has to go behind Thorin's back to do something he knows Thorin would hate—giving the Arkenstone to Bard—but he does it for the greater good of peace. Have you ever done something you knew someone you cared about would not like, but for a greater cause? What was it? Was it difficult to do? How did the other person react when they found out?

8. Thorin says to Bilbo, "If more of us valued food and cheer and song above hoarded gold, it would be a merrier world." Do you agree with this? Have you seen this in others' lives? That is, have you known people who clearly value the first above the second or the second above the first? If so, what are they and their lives like?

Workbook Answers

8.1.L IDENTIFYING CONFLICT (5 POINTS POSSIBLE)

1. Character versus character
2. Character versus nature
3. Character versus society
4. Character versus character
5. Character versus self

8.2.L CHARACTER VERSUS NATURE (5 POINTS POSSIBLE)

Students' answers will vary. All that is important is they give five examples and each example be of the appropriate type.

8.3.L CHARACTER VERSUS CHARACTER (5 POINTS POSSIBLE)

Students' answers will vary. All that is important is they give five examples and each example be of the appropriate type.

8.4.L CHARACTER VERSUS SOCIETY (5 POINTS POSSIBLE)

Students' answers will vary. All that is important is they give five examples and each example be of the appropriate type.

8.5.L CHARACTER VERSUS SELF (5 POINTS POSSIBLE)

Students' answers will vary. All that is important is they give five examples and each example be of the appropriate type.

8.6.G CAPITALIZATION (28 POINTS POSSIBLE)

J.R.R. Tolkien didn't just write wonderful novels, he also invented whole languages. **P**erhaps thinking that the languages he spoke, such as **F**innish, **W**elsh, and **O**ld **E**nglish, weren't enough, he invented **Q**uenya, **S**indarin, and **K**huzdul, among others. **T**hese languages are all part of **M**iddle **E**arth and spoken by its various inhabitants. **M**any of the languages **T**olkien created are various forms of the major language **E**lvish. **D**warves spoke **K**huzdul though. **O**rcs also had their own tongue called, appropriately enough, **O**rkish. **E**lves don't exist, as far as we know, but that hasn't stopped people from studying **E**lvish. **W**ho knows? **M**aybe one of those students of **E**lvish will run into **E**lrond someday and be ready for a glorious conversation.

This exercise may confuse some students a bit because so many of the words that require capitalization are the names of fake languages. You can point out to them that, just as fictitious character names are capitalized, so are the names of fictitious languages.

8.7.T FACT AND OPINION (17 POINTS POSSIBLE)

It's a Mystery to Me

I think murder mysteries should be taught in schools. <u>We shouldn't remove necessary courses like literature, math, and science; but we should add to this with a class in the murder mystery.</u> <u>Murder mysteries can teach a lot about English, history, and thinking skills.</u>

<u>Many murder mysteries are very well written and can teach a lot about plot, character, and setting.</u> <u>Mystery plots are wonderfully complicated and intriguing.</u> <u>Their rich characters run a wide range from the heroic detective to the evil murderer.</u> And some mysteries are series where the same characters appear again and again, giving the writer even more time to develop them. Mysteries are often set in exotic places, whether its a gothic English mansion or an archeological dig in Egypt. <u>Mystery writers bring their skills to all these areas, and we could learn a great deal about writing from reading them.</u>

Several mysteries are historic in nature, either because the writer set them in historic times or because they were written long enough ago that they are historic to us now. In particular, there are many mysteries set in historic England. From medieval to Victorian times and beyond, England has been a favorite setting for mysteries. <u>We could learn so much about that country just by reading its mysteries, which would be so much more fun than reading dull textbooks.</u>

<u>But the best use of murder mysteries in schools would be to improve students' thinking skills.</u> Some mysteries, such as the Sherlock Holmes stories of Sir Arthur Conan Doyle, give you all the clues you need to solve the mystery. <u>Having children read these stories, but stopping before the end, and giving their best guess as to identity of the murderer, would be a wonderful way to improve their logical and deductive powers.</u> They would then read the end of the story and discover if they were right or wrong.

<u>There are so many uses for murder mysteries in school, I don't know why a Murder Mystery 101 isn't required across the country.</u> <u>English, history, and thinking skills are three of the most vital subjects, and why we ignore such a fun way to teach them is a mystery to me.</u>

1. This article contains more opinions.

2. Student answers will vary. The writer might be able to find some examples of teachers using this method and quote that information here. The writer might even conduct an experiment with a classroom or another group of children and discuss the results.

3. The one specific example the author gives is of Sherlock Holmes. Yes, giving more specific examples would help. First, it would demonstrate a greater depth of thought on the author's part about the topic. Second, it would give anyone wishing to follow this suggestion a starting point for some mysteries to use. (For example, if I wish to teach my students about medieval England using mysteries, what authors and/or titles do I look for?) Third, it always strengthens an argument to provide specific examples for support. (The student need only give one of these reasons, or a similarly sensible reason, for full credit.)

4. The words *I think* are unnecessary in the first sentence.

8.8.A ANALYZING LITERATURE (8 POINTS POSSIBLE)

1. In the first three paragraphs Jenny experiences a conflict with society.

2. In the last paragraph Jenny experiences a character vs character conflict.

3. The word *comely* means attractive or beautiful.

4. Jenny wears a silk dress in public.

5. The two best answers here are description and the opinion of others. Action is also an acceptable answer.

6. The two best answers here are action and speech, but description is also an acceptable answer.

8.9.P *THE HOBBIT* CROSSWORD PUZZLE

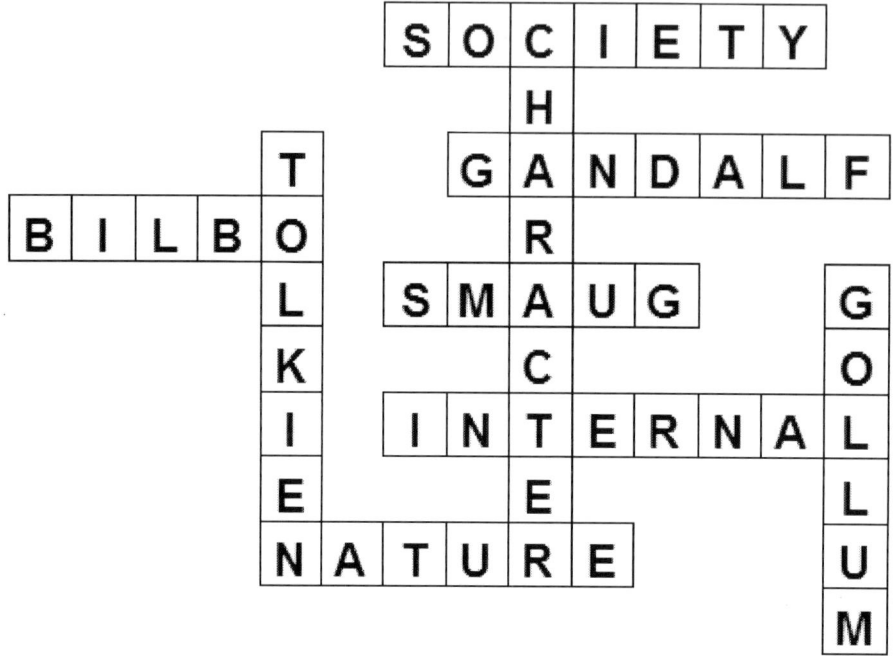

8.10.P *THE HOBBIT* WORD SEARCH

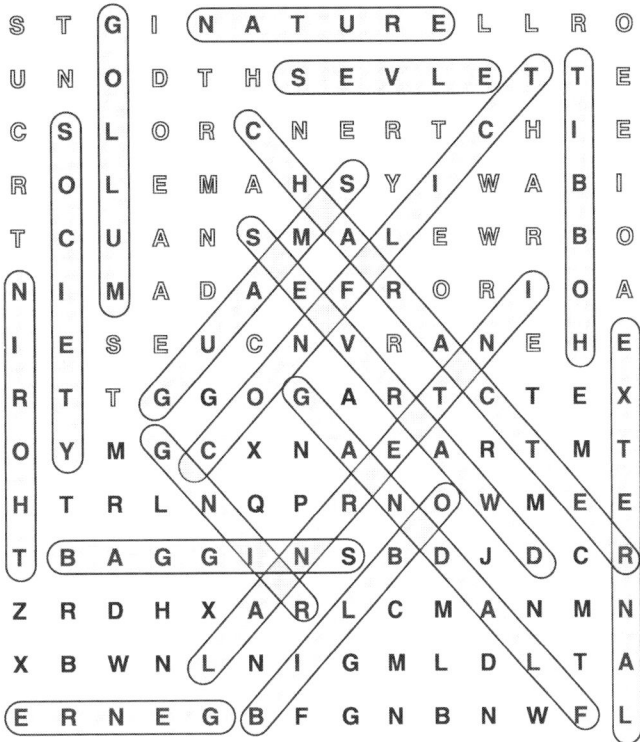

8.11.E THE FIVE-PARAGRAPH ESSAY

Answers will vary, but make sure the student has chosen a topic that is concise enough, and that the introductory paragraph includes three supporting details. Each of the next three paragraphs should take one of these supporting details and expand on it. The last paragraph should reiterate the information from the first paragraph but use different language.

Chapter Nine

"Reflections" by Lafcadio Hearn

Stories and Poems for Extremely Intelligent Children of All Ages—Pages 42 to 48

Student Guide—Pages 177 to 189

Workbook—Pages 187 to 210

Chapter 9: "Reflections"

Answers to Comprehension Questions

1. The father says his son must get married because he (the father) is getting older and when he dies the son will need someone to take care of him.

2. Student answers will vary a bit; good answers would be nervous, uncomfortable, shy, upset (for a moment).

3. Tassel suggests that her husband goes to Kioto because she is worried about him after his father dies, and she wants him to enjoy himself.

4. The young man is astonished when he looks in the mirror because he sees his father there.

5. The salesman wished he had asked more for the mirror because the young man was so eager to pay what he asked, and the salesman knew he would have paid more.

6. The young man made the mistake of not telling his wife about the mirror.

7. When Tassel looks in the cupboard she thinks her husband is keeping a woman there.

8. The Lady Abbess settles the dispute.

Literary Lesson: Symbolism

If your student grasped the chapter on figurative language, they will probably have no trouble here. Like figurative language, symbolism is the representation of one thing for another. Although I discuss *A Christmas Carol* in the lesson, if your student is having trouble with symbolism, you might want to read parts of this book together, particularly the descriptions of the three spirits and Jacob Marley's ghost. Discuss the symbolism together. If your student enjoyed the story by Lafcadio Hearn, there is another in *Stories and Poems*, "The Spring Lover and the Autumn Lover" beginning on p. 261. This story also contains symbolism.

Mini-Lesson: Sentence Structure

Although this program is not meant to be a grammar program, I decided to include a lesson on sentence structure because it is such a common problem for high-school students. This leads me to the conclusion that most grammar programs do not teach this subject well enough. There is no guarantee that I have done a better job here, but it can help students to read about something several times and from different authors.

Writing Exercises

The first exercise allows students to draw from their own lives. The second is for students who like writing stories. The third allows students to take the knowledge gained from an earlier lesson and apply it to the story they just read, through analysis. This is probably the most challenging of the four exercises. The final choice is a research paper, though it still requires the student to address the topic of symbolism.

Discussion Questions

1. What did you learn about Japanese culture from this story? Did it make you want to learn more about this culture, either present or past?

2. If you were to look into a mirror now in the same way the characters in the story did, what do you think you'd see there? That is, what is your heart full of at the moment that would be reflected by this mirror?

Workbook Answers

9.1.L RECOGNIZING SYMBOLS (12 POINTS POSSIBLE)

Note that the answers for numbers 3, 6, and 9 will vary. I have supplied some likely answers. What's most important though is that students are able to reasonably explain the answer. That is, they need to explain how the symbol might reasonably symbolize the abstract quality they've attached to it. (If you need further help with this, look at the example on the workbook page itself.)

1. The pocket-watch is probably a symbol.

2. We know it is probably a symbol because the character reacts so strongly to it.

3. The watch might be symbolic of a broken friendship or romance between Charles and the woman. Or it might be symbolic of someone who has died. The reason for this is the character bursts into tears when she sees it. Another good answer would be that the watch is symbolic of something about time (a time in the girl's life, a time past that can never be regained, etc.).

4. The horse figurines are probably symbolic.

5. We know they are symbolic because they appear repeatedly in the story.

6. The horses could be symbolic of a sense of freedom or power, because those qualities are often associated with horses.

7. The red dress is probably a symbol.

8. Two answers are possible here: We know it may be a symbol because the character is attaching unusual importance to it. We also know it may be a symbol because its color is red, a common symbolic color.

9. The dress may be a symbol of an event that happened long ago involving Margaret because she is wearing it for a particular occasion that could be related to that event somehow (like its anniversary). The dress could also be symbolic of danger or excitement or wrong-doing, as the color red is strongly associated with these things.

10. Mr. Fear is probably a symbol.

11. He is probably a symbol because of his name.

12. He is symbolic of Beryl's fear. We know this because of his name and the way that Beryl thinks of him is the same as one experiences fear.

9.2.L CREATING YOUR OWN SYMBOLS (10 POINTS POSSIBLE)

Student answers will vary. Students can use any symbols they want; the important thing is that their explanations tie them to the abstract qualities.

9.3.M FIXING INCOMPLETE SENTENCES 1 (10 POINTS POSSIBLE)

Answers will vary. All that's important is that students create complete sentences, but not run-on sentences or comma splices.

9.4.M FIXING INCOMPLETE SENTENCES 2 (10 POINTS POSSIBLE)

Answers will vary. All that's important is that students create complete sentences, but not run-on sentences or comma splices.

9.5.M FIXING RUN-ON SENTENCES (11 POINTS POSSIBLE)

Answers will vary. The important part is the run-on sentences are fixed properly. This can be done by creating two sentences, separating the clauses with a semicolon, or adding a conjunction. The answers I give here are all separated by periods just to show you where each independent clauses lie. But students may choose a semicolon or a conjunction instead of a period.

1. Japan is made up of thousands of islands. Honshu, Hokkaido, Kyushu, and Shikoku are the biggest.

2. Japan has about as much land as California. Well over half of this land is mountainous.

3. Japan has many volcanoes. The most famous of these is Mt. Fuji.

4. Mt. Fuji is one of the most beautiful mountains in the world. It is considered holy by some people.

5. In Japanese, the name of the country is Nippon. It is also called "Land of the Rising Sun."

6. In the Middle Ages, the samurai appeared. These were Japanese warriors.

7. There are many great samurai movies. *The Seven Samurai* is probably the most famous and certainly one of the best.

8. *The Magnificent Seven* is an American western heavily based on *The Seven Samurai*. Several American westerns are essentially remakes of Japanese samurai movies.

9. Most Japanese people are Shinto or Buddhist. A minority of people in Japan belong to other religions.

10. Modern Japan has an elected Parliament and a Prime Minster. There is still an emperor too. He holds no real power. (Note that this is three sentences, not just two. This questions is worth two points.)

9.6.A ANALYZING LITERATURE (12 POINTS POSSIBLE)

1. The yellow wallpaper is probably a symbol.

2. The three indications that the wallpaper is symbolic are (1) the fact that it is the title of the story, (2) its frequent appearance in the story (although the student has not read the whole story, they should be able to tell that two long descriptions of wallpaper in a short story is a bit much), and (3) the character's overly strong reaction to it.

3. Student must name three of the following: (1) the garden, (2) arbors, (3) flowers, (4) bushes, (5) trees, (6) the bay, (7) a private wharf, (8) a shaded lane. Another possible answer is people walking, but it is unclear if she actually sees them or only imagines them.

4. Gilman uses action and the opinion of others to develop the narrator's character.

5. Gilman uses personification several times to describe the wallpaper. Student must give one of the following examples: (1) When you follow the lame uncertain curves for a little distance they suddenly commit suicide; destroy themselves in unheard of contradictions; (2) this paper looks to me as if it knew what a vicious influence it had; (3) there is a recurrent spot where the pattern lolls like a broken neck and two bulbous eyes stare at you upside down; (4) up and down and sideways they crawl, and (5) those absurd, unblinking eyes are everywhere.

   Gilman probably chose to use personification to make the wallpaper seem more alive, hence creepier, and to give the story an eerier tone (as that is the effect it has here).

9.7.P "REFLECTIONS" CROSSWORD PUZZLE

9.8.P "Reflections" Word Search

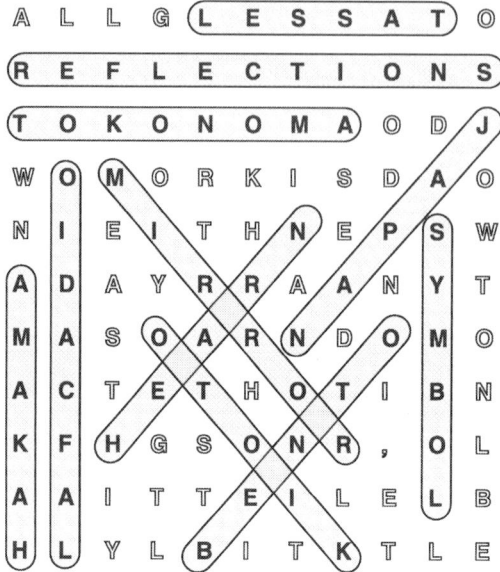

9.9.E Expository Essay

Answers will vary, but make sure the student has chosen a topic that is concise enough and either (1) gives information, (2) defines an idea, or (3) explains a topic. The introductory paragraph includes three supporting details. Each of the next three paragraphs should take one of these supporting details and expand on it. The last paragraph should reiterate the information from the first paragraph but use different language.

Chapter Ten

My Family and Other Animals by Gerald Durrell

NOTE: This book contains mild swearing. If this concerns you, you may want to read the book first and eliminate certain sections from your child's assigned reading or talk about it with you child.

Student Guide—Pages 191 to 215

Workbook—Pages 211 to 230

Chapter 10: *My Family and Other Animals*

Answers to Comprehension Questions

THE SPEECH FOR THE DEFENSE
1. The author was ten when his family went to Corfu.

PART ONE
THE MIGRATION
1. The family moves from England.
2. Judging by her luggage, Margo's primary concern is her appearance.
3. Judging by his luggage, the author's primary interest is animals.
4. Durrell uses personification here.

1: THE UNSUSPECTED ISLE
1. Roger the dog keeps them from having a dignified entrance to Corfu.
2. Mother insists they find a house in the country because she finds the town very unhygienic and is worried about an epidemic.
3. None of the villas have bathrooms.

2: THE STRAWBERRY-PINK VILLA
1. Spiro acts as the family's guide, philosopher, and friend.
2. Larry's trunks are full of books.
3. Mother and Gerald (the author) are the two most interested in the garden.

3: THE ROSE-BEETLE MAN
1. Roger the dog is the author's companion.
2. The author and Agathi sing peasant songs together.
3. Yani warns the author against sleeping under cypress trees.
4. The author buys a tortoise whose favorite food is strawberries.

4: A BUSHEL OF LEARNING
1. Student must name at least two of the following: (1) to shoot, (2) to sail, (3) to dance, (4) mathematics, (5) French, (6) spelling, and (7) literature.
2. Gerry learns to observe and note down his observations in a diary.

3. Gerry's tutor tries to put animals into all the subjects that Gerry isn't naturally interested in (math, history, geography) to increase his interest.

5: A TREASURE OF SPIDERS

1. Gerry wants to wake Yani because he's hungry and knows that Yani will give him something to eat.

2. Student must name one of the following: (1) Theodore does not talk down to him, (2) he is a scientist, (3) he is the only person he has met who is as interested as he is in zoology, and (4) he takes time to send him a microscope and invite him to tea.

6: THE SWEET SPRING

1. Student must name two of the following: (1) Larry drank wine and sang love songs, (2) mother gardened and cooked more, (3) Margo became even more obsessed with her appearance and began dating a Turk, (4) Leslie bought a new gun and went shooting, and (5) the author (Gerry) is eager to explore nature more with Theodore.

CONVERSATION

1. Answers will vary, but saying that the family will move shows the greatest insight on the student's part.

Part Two

7: THE DAFFODIL-YELLOW VILLA

1. The gardener and his wife live there.

2. Talking about her health problems is the only thing that makes Lugaretzia happy.

3. In this sentence, the author uses personification.

4. Margo kisses the Saint's feet hopping he'll cure her acne, but instead she comes down with the flu.

8: THE TORTOISE HILLS

1. Gerry sees a tortoise emerging out of the earth.

2. The male tortoises fight over mates.

3. Gerry collects an egg.

4. The author is using a simile.

9: THE WORLD IN A WALL

1. The scorpion is the most dangerous inhabitant of the wall.

2. Gerry smuggles in a scorpion mother and her babies.

3. Student must name one of the following: (1) Larry develops a phobia about match-boxes; (2) Lugaretzia is bitten by Roger, and long after her ankle is healed she continues to bandage it, limp, and show it to everyone; and (3) Mother decides that Gerry is running wild again and needs another tutor.

4. During their French lessons, the Belgian consul shoots cats. He does this because they breed unchecked in this part of town and none of them are cared for so they become very sick and malnourished.

10: THE PAGEANT OF FIREFLIES

1. Gerry works on a book, writing every day, and Peter corrects what he writes.

2. Gerry is forced to get rid of his stuffed bat.

3. Ulysses is an owl that Gerry brings home with him and keeps.

4. Mother buys a bathing suit.

11: THE ENCHANTED ARCHIPELAGO

1. All of the birthday gifts Gerry asks for relate to his nature exploration and collection.

2. Leslie builds a boat for Gerry for his birthday.

3. As soon as its mast is put in, the Bootle-Bumtrinket capsizes.

4. The family had agreed to invite only ten guests, but each member of the family invited their own ten (all being different except for Theodore), so they ended up inviting 46 people.

12: THE WOODCOCK WINTER

1. Margo is upset because Peter has been sent away.

2. Margo has difficulty rowing back from the island because she had fallen asleep in the sun and gotten a terrible burn that has swelled her eyes nearly shut. (Another possible answer is that the seas have gotten stormy, though that is not the primary cause of her trouble.)

3. Durrell is using personification.

4. Leslie enjoyed winter on the island because it was hunting time, and Leslie loved to hunt.

5. Larry is always telling people that he could easily do whatever they do, though he never actually does these things.

CONVERSATION

No Comprehension Questions

Part Three

13: THE SNOW-WHITE VILLA

1. Geronimo is a gecko that lives in Gerry's room.

2. Cicely is a praying mantis that Gerry has captured. She has a fight with Geronimo which she loses.

3. Gerry shows Spiro two large toads.

14: THE TALKING FLOWERS

1. Student answers will vary a bit, but should say something about Gerry's attitude being poor or Gerry being disgruntled or unhappy.

2. Gerry's family tells him the new tutor is interested in birds. Gerry does not believe them, but they prove to be correct.

3. Gerry thinks his tutor is being extremely polite about having to go to the toilet.

4. Mrs. Kralefsky uses a simile.

15: THE CYCLAMEN WOODS

1. Larry's objection to the magpies is that they'll steal.

2. The magpies attack Larry's room, so Gerry has to build a cage for them.

3. Gerry wants Mr. Kralefsky to teach him wrestling because he believes one of the tales that Mr. Kralefsky tells him in which he beats someone at wrestling.

16: THE LAKE OF LILIES

1. Mother brings the newest pet to the household.

2. Dodo's hip goes out of the socket, causing her to shriek periodically.

3. Answers will vary; the answer must be a sentence or phrase from the description of the Lake of Lilies that addresses any sense other than sight. (Sight can be included too, but one other sense must be there.)

17: THE CHESSBOARD FIELDS

1. Gerry catches two snakes instead.

2. Gerry meets a convict and receives a gull from him. Gerry is thrilled to get the gull.

3. Larry has the worst reaction to Alecko.

18: AN ENTERTAINMENT WITH ANIMALS

1. Gerry has to separate the goldfish from the reptiles because the reptiles begin eating the goldfish.

2. Student must name two of the following: (1) the magpies attack the table, (2) dogs try to get at Dodo, (3) snakes in the bath scare Leslie, (4) Alecko bites people, and (5) a dog fight breaks out in the house.

THE RETURN

1. The family has to leave Corfu because Gerry needs to go elsewhere to finish his education.

Literary Lesson: Humor

Probably the most difficult concept in this lesson is irony. Usually students will learn more about irony in high-school as well; this is just to give an introduction to it. Very few students will become highly competent at writing humor, since very few people in general do. My hope is that they will get a bit better at it, and use it to spice up their writing here and there. I also hope they will learn to identify it and appreciate it more in literature. There is little more depressing as a teacher than to have a student who completely misses the humor of a piece and takes a writer seriously or literally who never meant to be taken that way.

My trinity of humorists consists of Mark Twain, P. G. Wodehouse, and James Thurber. Not all of Twain's writing is humor, though much of it is. Virtually all of Wodehouse and Thurber is humorous, though some will not be understood by junior high students as it deals with specific topics they would be unfamiliar with.

The Adventures of Huckleberry Finn is Twain's masterpiece; it is used in the American Literature, Mid–Late 19th-Century, Lightning Lit Guide. (That chapter is on humor as well.) Twain has several humorous short stories, including one in *Stories and Poems*. Twain is particularly good for examining exaggeration, understatement, and dialect. I think the best Wodehouse novels are those that take place in Blandings Castle, though other people prefer the Jeeves and Wooster series. Either would be a good start. He also has written many funny short stories and essays. Wodehouse's humor relies heavily on under-statement, caricature, and misunderstandings. His humor is also very English, and I'm uncertain how much of it might go over the heads of American junior-high students. Thurber has many short pieces. "The Secret Life of Walter Mitty" is the introduction to Thurber for many people, and it is an appropriate piece for junior-high students. Thurber also wrote many humorous pieces about dogs, and these would also be a wonderful place to start. Thurber's humor may be the hardest of the three for students to analyze, but might be some of the easiest for them to enjoy.

Mini-Lesson: Bibliography

The most important point of this mini-lesson is that every paper that requires research in any class also requires a bibliography. It is also good for students to begin to learn the proper formatting, though there are so many little rules to this that I don't expect anything near perfection here. It's perfectly fine for students to refer to handbooks for help with formatting a bibliography all through high-school and college. They should be able to remember some basic things like what information is needed (so they'll remember to write it down in their notes), that the entries are alphabetized, and that each ends with a period. The order of the information and other punctuation can be found in a style guide, especially for sources that aren't used as often such as books with translators or interviews. It is important after this point that you always require your students to include a properly formatted bibliography for any paper requiring research in any class.

Writing Exercises

The first two exercises allow students to draw from their own lives and practice using some humorous techniques. The third is an analysis; none of these is necessarily any harder than the other, it will depend more on the student's ability and interests. The fourth is the research paper, which can now be complete (since the student now knows how to do a bibliography).

Discussion Questions

1. Gerry is fascinated, almost obsessed, with nature. It is his passion. Is there anything you feel this passionate about, anything that you could spend hours doing? Gerry's love as a boy grew into his career as an adult. Is there a chance that your passion could as well? In what way could it become a career?

2. The family members each have very different personalities. Which one reminds you most of you? Why? Which one (they may not be the same) would you most want to spend time with? Why?

3. The family picks up and moves someplace entirely new, someplace they've never been before. Have you ever done that? How was the experience? If you haven't, do you think it is something you would like to do? If you could choose anywhere in the world to move to, where would you choose?

4. What is your relationship with and attitude towards nature like? In what ways is it like Gerry's? In what ways is it different?

5. Gerry and Theodore have a relationship of great respect based on their mutual love of nature. Have you ever had a relationship with an adult like this? What was your connection with this person? How was it different from most of your relationships with adults?

Workbook Answers

10.1.L IDENTIFYING METHODS OF HUMOR (11 POINTS POSSIBLE)

1. Mistake
2. Sarcasm
3. Understatement
4. Physical humor
5. Sarcasm
6. Mistake
7. Exaggeration
8. Physical humor
9. Exaggeration
10. Understatement and physical humor

10.2.L CREATING HUMOR (8 POINTS POSSIBLE)

Answers will vary. Don't knock a student too much for unfunny answers, but it's fine to do some brainstorming together to come up with funnier ones, especially if a student shows a talent for humor and just struggles with a few of these. More important than how funny the answers are is that each uses the proper technique.

10.3.M CORRECTING A BIBLIOGRAPHY (20 POINTS POSSIBLE)

"Biography: The Life of Paul Laurence Dunbar." 3 Feb. 2003. University of
    Dayton, Paul Laurence Dunbar Website. 2 July 2003
    <http://www.plethoreum.org/dunbar/>. [Quotes missing after Dunbar in
    first line, url missing, entry does not end in a period]

"Biography: Stephen Crane." Pearson Education, Inc. 19 July 2003
    <http://occawlonline.pearsoned.com/bookbind/pubbooks/kennedycompa
    ct_awl/chapter14/objectives/deluxe-content.html>. [Opening quote
    missing, period missing after Crane in first line]

Campbell, Donna M. "Realism in American Literature, 1860–1890." 5 April
    2003. Literary Movements. 27 July 2003
    <http://www.gonzaga.edu/faculty/campbell/enl311/realism.htm>.
    [Period missing after first 2003, date website was accessed is missing]

"The Collection: Selected Poems by Paul Laurence Dunbar." 3 Feb. 2003.
    University of Dayton, Paul Laurence Dunbar Website. 2 July 2003
    <http://www.plethoreum.org/dunbar/gallery.asp>. [Period missing after
    2003 in first line, > is missing after the url, entry does not end with a
    period.]

Cunliff, Marcus. *The Literature of the United States.* New York: Penguin Books,
    1986. [Publication city missing, comma missing after Penguin Books.]

Davis, Linda H. *Badge of Courage: the Life of Stephen Crane.* New York:
    Houghton Mifflin Co., 1998. [Order is wrong (this entry comes before
    "Gentry"), period missing after the author's middle initial, publisher name
    missing, entry does not end with a period.]

Gentry, Tony. *Paul Laurence Dunbar.* New York: Chelsea House Publisher,
    1989. [Period missing after book title, colon missing after New York.]

Ruland, Richard and Bradbury, Malcolm. *From Puritanism to Postmodernism:
    A History of American Literature.* New York: Viking, 1991. [Colon missing
    after New York, comma missing after Viking.]

10.4.M CREATING A BIBLIOGRAPHY

Barfield, Owen. *History in English Words.* Barrington, Mass.: Lindisfarne Books, 1967.

Eco, Umberto. "Casablanca, or, The Cliches are Having a Ball." *Porta Ludovica.* October 1995. The Modern Word. 3 April 2006 <http://www.themodernword.com/eco/eco_casablanca.html>.

_____. *Six Walks in the Fictional Woods.* Cambridge, Mass.: Harvard University Press, 1995.

_____. *Umberto Eco on Literature.* Orlando, Fla.: Harcourt Books, 2004.

Zinsser, William. *On Writing Well.* New York: HarperCollins, 1998.

10.5.A ANALYZING LITERATURE (8 POINTS POSSIBLE)

1. Student must name one of the following: (1) his own appearance, (2) modern photography, (3) photographs of authors on books, (4) photography of the past, and (5) his family's physical appearance.

2. In the opening paragraph Wodehouse uses physical humor and exaggeration.

3. Exaggeration is Wodehouse's primary technique in this essay.

4. Wodehouse is using a simile.

5. Wodehouse is implying that the second photograph is more attractive because it shows less of his uncle.

6. The author's purpose is to entertain.

10.6.P *MY FAMILY AND OTHER ANIMALS* CROSSWORD PUZZLE

```
                                    E
   C                      S         X
   O           S          A         A
   R           P          R         G
   F           I          C         G
U  N  D  E  R  S  T  A  T  E  M  E  N  T
   U           O          S         R
   R                      M         A
M  A  R  G  O                       T
   E                                I
   L  A  R  R  Y                    O
   L                                N
```

10.7.P *My Family and Other Animals* Word Search

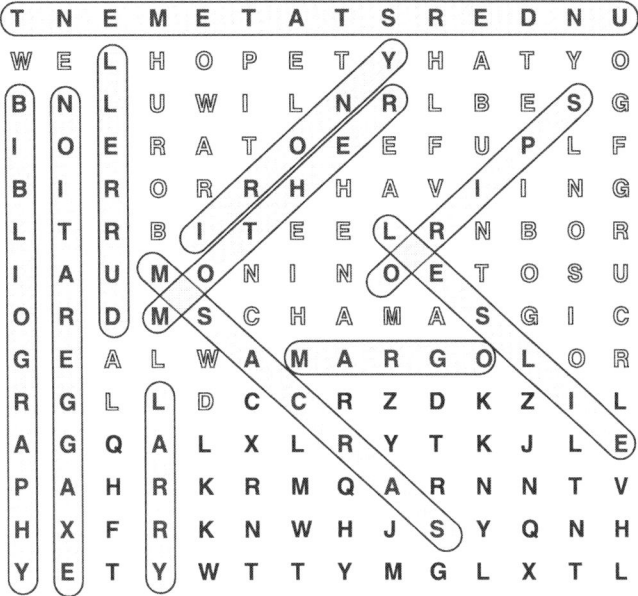

10.8.E Narrative Essay

Answers will vary.

Chapter Eleven

Meter in Poetry

Stories and Poems for Extremely Intelligent Children of All Ages

Student Guide—Pages 217 to 238

Workbook—Pages 231 to 249

Chapter 11: Meter in Poetry

Answers to Comprehension Questions

"THE HUMAN SEASONS"

1. Keats uses the four seasons (spring, summer, fall, and winter) as a metaphor for various times in a person's life.

2. According to Keats, a man's "fair spring thoughts" become a part of him in the summer of his life.

3. Winter keeps man from forgetting that he is mortal.

"THE FAIRIES"

1. Student must name one of the following: (1) a green jacket, (2) a red cap, (3) a white owl's feather.

2. The old King sits on the hill-top.

3. Bridget was stolen by the fairies for seven years, then she died of sorrow.

4. He probably dug up one of the thorn-trees.

"I LOVED A LASS"

1. Wither uses a simile.

2. The speaker's primary emotion is sadness.

"THE SPLENDOUR FALLS ON CASTLE WALLS"

1. The sense of hearing is also addressed in this poem.

"SO, WE'LL GO NO MORE A-ROVING"

1. The speaker means he has gotten old.

"A WINTRY SONNET"

1. The ocean remains disappointed (thirsty).

"NIGHTMARE"

1. Gilbert is using personification.

"MARIANA"

1. This poem is set on a farm.

2. c and d are both acceptable answers

Literary Lesson: Meter in Poetry

Meter is usually the most difficult topic in poetry for students (of any age) to understand. This lesson is a brief and, I hope, kind introduction to the topic. There is some fairly technical vocabulary that I ask students to memorize, but I tried to keep it to a minimum. I think it is important and helpful for students to do this; once a student gets a strong handle on some of the impressive technical words it can give them a greater sense of confidence about the subject. The ideas really aren't difficult, but there are many aspects to meter and it can be confusing. Getting a strong grasp of a few of the ideas helps make the topic seem less threatening.

The first topic I discuss is the syllable. By eighth grade many students will already know what syllables are. If you have a student who does not, and who struggles with the idea after reading the lesson, you can try teaching syllables by tapping them out with words on a table. Start with two- and three-syllable words first, as these are usually the best for introducing the concept.

The next topic is stress. Some students will already know about stress, others will understand it very quickly, and some students have a terrible time hearing stress. I've seen a lot of variation in students' ability to understand this idea, and I don't know why this is (unless it has something to do with how auditory a student is). Sometimes the best way for a student to come to grips with stress in speech is to focus at first on those words which can be stressed in different places for different meanings. I give one example in the lesson of *RE-cord* and *re-CORD*. Others are:

CON-flict (I don't want to have a conflict with him.) and *con-FLICT* (Our schedules conflict.);
PER-mit (We need a permit to build there.) and *per-MIT* (I'm afraid I can't permit that.);
AD-dress (What is your current address.) and *ad-DRESS* (Please address this envelope.);
COM-bine (Farmer Brown bought a new combine.) and *com-BINE* (Please combine the ingredients before continuing.);
COM-press (Put a cold compress on your head.) and *com-PRESS* (Can you compress all those clothes into that suitcase?)
CON-tent (What are the contents of your purse?) and *con-TENT* (After such a good dinner, she was content.);

CON-tract (I won't sign the contract.) and *con-TRACT* (When did you contract the measles?);

CON-vict and *con-VICT* (The convict was convicted of larceny.);

DE-sert (The desert is hot but beautiful.) and de-SERT (He deserted his platoon.);

IN-sult (That remark was quite the insult.) and *in-SULT* (Don't insult your mother.);

OB-ject (What is that object?) and *ob-JECT* (Do you object to this hat?);

PER-fect (That's the perfect dress for tonight.) and *perFECT* (Can you perfect this recipe?)

AT-tribute (He has many positive attributes.) and *At-TRIBute* (To what do you attribute your success?);

There are many others, but I hope this will be enough for any student who is having trouble.

From here on, the lesson gets more technical. If your student has trouble with this, I encourage you to read the lesson yourself and work on meter together. Choose other poems to examine. Nursery rhymes and limericks are often easily scanned. Also, feel free to contact me as well. One of the problems with meter, however, is it's a difficult thing to explain through simply writing. It's much easier if the teacher can actually be with the student, speaking and showing.

Mini-Lesson: The Sonnet

Most students understand rhyme schemes, so if the student can also grasp the idea of iambic pentameter, identifying sonnets should be no problem. If you wish to read more together, there are many on the web. Look for sonnets by William Shakespeare, John Donne, John Milton, William Wordsworth, Elizabeth Barrett Browning, John Keats, Percy Bysshe Shelley, Robert Frost, Edna St. Vincent Millay, and William Butler Yeats. (Of course, not all poems by these poets are sonnets, but all used the sonnet form at times.)

Writing Exercises

All too often in the high-school classes I have students who apparently think they've understood meter then attempt an exercise such as number 1, scanning a poem and writing about its meter. In examining their scansion, it becomes apparent that they still haven't learned about meter, in some cases not even about syllables. Trying this assignment is one way to see for certain how much your student understands about meter; it is not an easy assignment though.

The second assignment will also challenge a student's understanding of meter. The first assignment would be better for students who are more interested in analysis, while this one is meant for students who enjoy being more creative. The third and fourth assignments are similar, except in this case the metrical requirements have been imposed on the student.

The last assignment is for the student who still struggles greatly with meter. If your student is in this position by the end of the lesson and workbook pages, don't worry. Do try to be sure the student understands at least syllables and stress before leaving this lesson. Also, I think it's important for students to have the basic vocabulary I introduced. These basics are needed for trying meter again later. Meter is taught in some of the high-school Lightning Literature classes as well. It's very possible that with some more experience with poetry and maturity the 8th-grade student who couldn't grasp meter will become the 9th- or 10th-grade student who masters it easily. This assignment is also a good one if you wish to review all the aspects of poetry introduced in this course (and the 7th-grade course, if applicable), as it asks students to identify many aspects of the poem they've chosen as their favorite.

Discussion Questions

1. Do you think Keats's metaphor of seasons representing one's life is accurate? In what ways is it accurate and in what ways do you think it could be improved? As you are still in the "spring" of your life, might it be difficult for you to judge this right now?

2. Tennyson's poem describes a place that is beautiful but that has seen better days. Its largest glory was in the past. Do you know any place like that? Is there a place that is still beautiful but that you know, or imagine, was once even more beautiful? Where is it? Is it someplace you can go or only someplace you have heard about? If the latter, would you like to go there?

3. Like the characters in "A Wintry Sonnet," do you sometimes feel that winter will never end? You need not take this literally—a "winter" in our lives is sometimes a metaphor for bad times. Have you ever been in the middle of a difficult situation that you thought would never end? How did that feel? Did the situation eventually get better? What can you do to help prepare you for your next "winter" so you can remember better that "spring" will eventually come?

4. How do your nightmares, and your feelings during them, compare to those in Gilbert's poem? In what ways are they the same? In what ways are they different?

5. One critic has argued that Mariana (in the last poem) does not actually want the other person (whoever "he" is) to return, that she likes being

miserable. What do you think of this assessment of the poem? Can you see anything in the poem to support it or to argue against it?

6. Both Mariana and the speaker in "I Loved a Lass" have lost someone. Compare and contrast these two characters and their responses to a lost love. Can you relate to either one or the other more?

Workbook Answers

11.1.L MATCHING TERMS (9 POINTS POSSIBLE)

1. f.
2. d.
3. i.
4. g.
5. a.
6. c.
7. e.
8. b.
9. h.

11.2.L DEFINING TERMS (9 POINTS POSSIBLE)

Note: This workbook page is to help students assess how much of the vocabulary they have really learned. Any that they miss should be gone over before going on with more workbook pages, and they should study the words they missed until they have them all fully imbedded in their vocabulary.

1. An iamb is an unstressed syllable followed by a stressed syllable.

2. A trochee is a stressed syllable followed by an unstressed syllable.

3. A dactyl is a stressed syllable followed by two unstressed syllables.

4. An anapest is two unstressed syllables followed by a stressed syllable.

5. Trimeter means three feet per line.

6. Tetrameter means four feet per line.

7. Pentameter means five feet per line.

8. A scansion is an analysis of the meter of a poem done with certain markings.

9. A foot is a unit of (usually) two or three syllables.

11.3.L DEFINING THE SAME TERMS AGAIN (9 POINTS POSSIBLE)

This time, students are allowed to skip any terms that they correctly defined on their first attempt at workbook page 11.2.L. This page is meant to pick up any remaining terms they have not yet mastered.

1. An iamb is an unstressed syllable followed by a stressed syllable.
2. A trochee is a stressed syllable followed by an unstressed syllable.
3. A dactyl is a stressed syllable followed by two unstressed syllables.
4. An anapest is two unstressed syllables followed by a stressed syllable.
5. Trimeter means three feet per line.
6. Tetrameter means four feet per line.
7. Pentameter means five feet per line.
8. A scansion is an analysis of the meter of a poem done with certain markings.
9. A foot is a unit of (usually) two or three syllables.

11.4.L IDENTIFYING METER (20 POINTS POSSIBLE)

1. Iambic trimeter
2. Dactylic tetrameter
3. Trochaic tetrameter
4. Anapestic tetrameter
5. Iambic pentameter
6. Trochaic tetrameter
7. Iambic trimeter
8. Anapestic tetrameter
9. Iambic pentameter
10. Trochaic pentameter

11.5.A Analyzing Literature (67-71 points possible)

```
    ∪   /      ∪  ∪  /     ∪  ∪  /      ∪  ∪  /
1.  There lived | an old man | in the king | dom of Tess,

     ∪   ∪ /     ∪  ∪  /      ∪ ∪/     ∪∪    /
    Who invent | ed a pure | ly orig | inal dress;

     ∪    /     ∪  ∪  /      ∪∪  /      ∪  ∪    /
    And when | it was per | fectly made | and complete,

    ∪  /    ∪   ∪   /     ∪    /     / ∪   ∪    /
    He o| pened the door | and walked | into | the street.
```

(58 points for the scansion)

2. This poem's meter is anapestic tetrameter.

3. The most significant variation of this meter is with the words "and walked into the street." Lear probably chose variety here to emphasize the character's actions and the shift to the next part of the poem.

4. This poem is made up of couplets. (If your student has not taken Lightning Lit 7 and you have not previously studied couplets, you may drop this question.)

5. Lear gives the following details of sound: "a great noise / Of all sorts of Beasticles, Birdlings, and Boys," the screechings of cats, and a squall.

6. Lear gives one detail of touch: "The warmth of whose skins was quite fluffy and nice."

7. This poem is set mostly on a street (and partly in a home) in the Kingdom of Tess.

8. This word is a nonce word. (If your student has not taken Lightning Lit 7 and you have not previously studied nonce words, you may drop this question.)

9. Lear is using alliteration. (If your student has not taken Lightning Lit 7 and you have not previously studied alliteration you may drop this question.)

10. Lear is using assonance. (If your student has not taken Lightning Lit 7 and you have not previously studied assonance, you may drop this question.)

11. Lear primarily uses physical humor.

11.6.P METER IN POETRY CROSSWORD PUZZLE

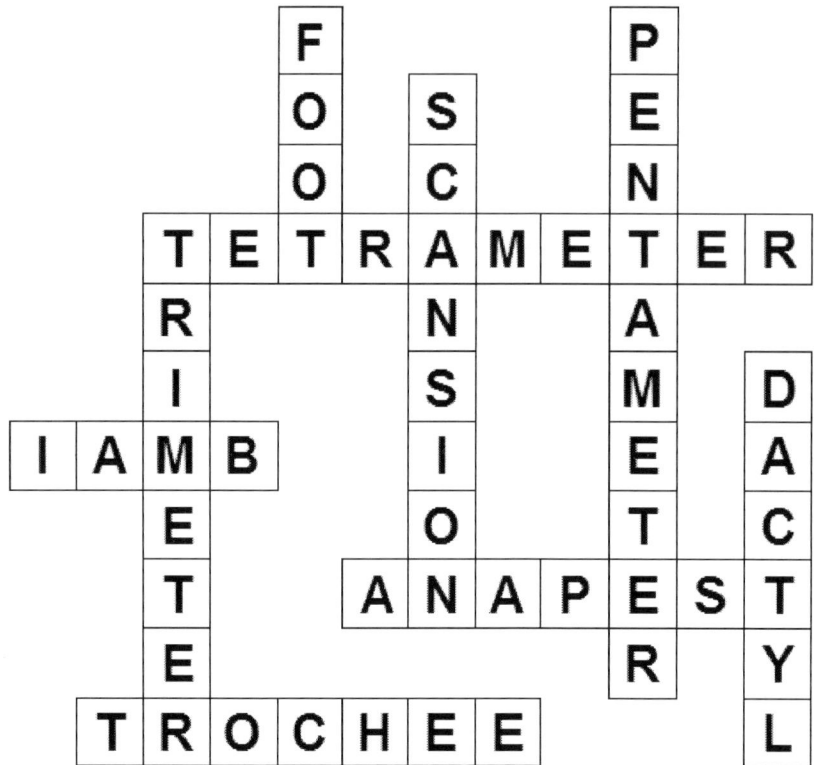

11.7.P METER IN POETRY WORD SEARCH

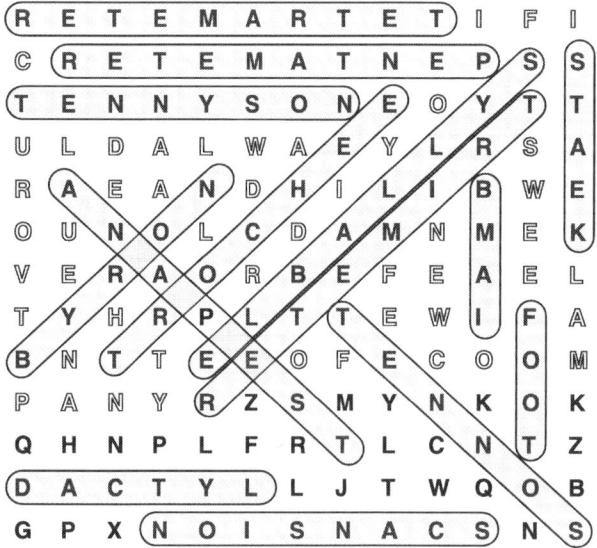

11.8.E Audio Sonnets

Remember that scansion is an art, not a science. A student's answer may differ somewhat from this one, but should not differ too radically.

Sonnet 60   (144 POINTS POSSIBLE)

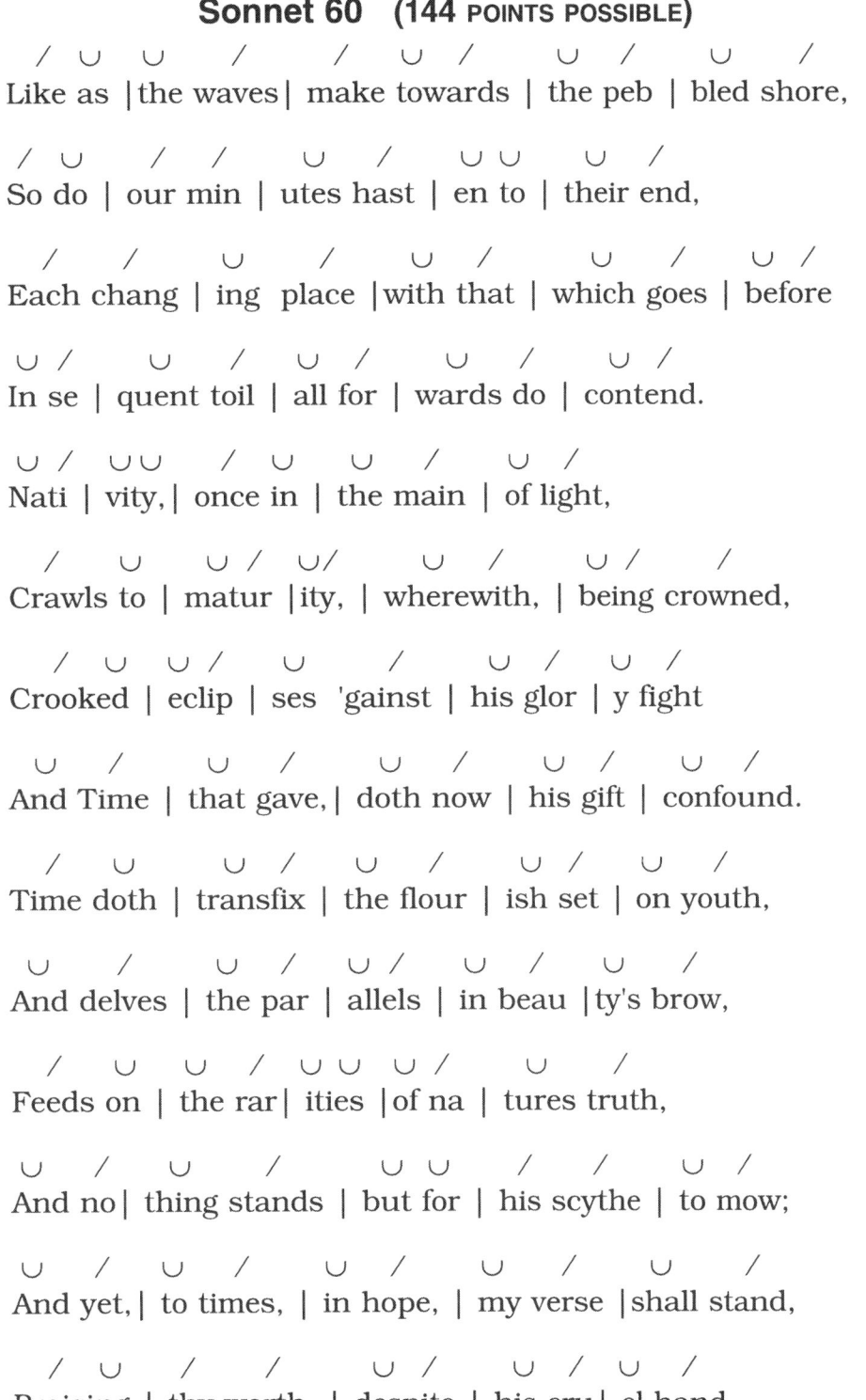

Like as |the waves| make towards | the peb | bled shore,

So do | our min | utes hast | en to | their end,

Each chang | ing place |with that | which goes | before

In se | quent toil | all for | wards do | contend.

Nati | vity,| once in | the main | of light,

Crawls to | matur |ity, | wherewith, | being crowned,

Crooked | eclip | ses 'gainst | his glor | y fight

And Time | that gave,| doth now | his gift | confound.

Time doth | transfix | the flour | ish set | on youth,

And delves | the par | allels | in beau |ty's brow,

Feeds on | the rar| ities |of na | tures truth,

And no| thing stands | but for | his scythe | to mow;

And yet,| to times, | in hope, | my verse |shall stand,

Praising | thy worth, | despite | his cru| el hand.

Sonnet 116 (200 POINTS POSSIBLE)

```
 /   U    /   U    U   /    U    U    /    /
Let me | not to | the mar | riage of | true minds

 U   /    U   /    U   U     /   U    U   /
Admit | imped | iments. | Love is | not love

  U   /    U   /    U  /   U /   U   /
Which al | ters when | it al | tera | tion finds,

 U   /     U   U    U  /    U  U   U  /
Or bends | with the | remov | er to | remove:

 U   /    /  U    U  /    U  /    U   /
O, no! | it is | an ev | er-fix | ed mark,

   U   /     U   /    U   U    U  /    U  /  U
That looks | on tem | pests and | is ne | ver shaken;

 /  U   U   /    U  /    U   /    U U   /
It is | the star | to ev | ery wan | dering bark,

   U     /      U   /     U   /     U   /     U  /  U
Whose worth's | unknown, | although | his height | be taken.

  /   U    /    /    U   /    U /    U    /
Love's not | Time's fool, | though ro | sy lips | and cheeks

  U   /    U   /    U   /    U    /    U   /
Within | his ben | ding sic | kle's com | pass come;

  /   /    U   /    U   /    /    /    U   /
Love al | ters not | with his | brief hours | and weeks,

  U    /    U   /   / U    U   U   /    U   /
But bears | it out | even | to the edge | of doom.

 U   /    U   /    U   U   U  /    U    /
If this | be er | ror and | upon | me prov'd,

 U   /    U    /    U   /    /   /    U   /
I ne | ver writ, | nor no | man ev | er lov'd.
```

[Editor's Note: This sonnet was featured in the movie *Sense and Sensibility* which has an interesting section on reading the

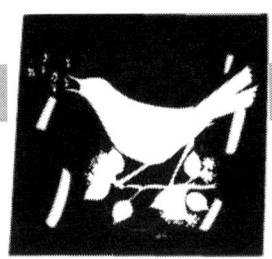

Chapter Twelve

To Kill a Mockingbird by Harper Lee

NOTE: This book contains mild swearing. If this concerns you, you may want to read the book first and eliminate certain sections from your child's assigned reading or talk about it with you child.

Student Guide—Pages 239 to 266

Workbook—Pages 251 to 277

Answers to Comprehension Questions

PART ONE

Chapter 1

1. The narrator is referring to The Civil War.
2. This story is set in Maycomb, Alabama.
3. Dill first gets the idea of making Boo Radley come out.
4. Mr. Radley kept Boo in the house for the next fifteen years.
5. Boo stabbed his father with a pair of scissors.
6. Jem's description of Boo Radley is most likely very inaccurate. There are two reasons for this (the student can give either or both): (1) Jem hasn't seen Boo for years and barely remembers the one time he did see him; (2) the whole town, including Jem, has created many superstitions about Boo, and Jem's description has much more to do with those superstitions than anything factual.

Chapter 2

1. Scout's teacher discovers Scout can read and does not like that.
2. Miss Caroline wants Scout's father to stop teaching Scout.
3. Walter Cunningham does not have a lunch because he is poor, and he refuses Miss Caroline's quarter for the same reason.

Chapter 3

1. Scout criticizes the way Walter eats.
2. At the beginning of her first day of school, Scout is eager for school and thrilled to be there; but by the end of the same day, she is dreading the next nine months.
3. Bob Ewell is allowed to hunt out of season because he spends his money on liquor rather than providing food for his children. So the people and the law allow him to hunt year-round so his children get something to eat.
4. Scout and Atticus agree that Scout will go to school and she and Atticus will continue to read every night.

Chapter 4

1. Scout is suspicious about the gum at first because she finds it in the tree at the Radley house.

2. The second thing Scout finds is a box with two Indian-head pennies in it.

3. Jem, Dill, and Scout play at being the Radleys.

4. Scout hears laughter coming from inside the house.

Chapter 5

1. Scout starts spending time with Miss Maudie because Jem and Dill start to exclude her.

2. Atticus interrupts Scout, Jem, and Dill.

Chapter 6

1. Student must name one of the following: (1) nobody could see them at night, (2) Atticus would be reading so wouldn't notice anything, (3) if Boo Radley killed them they would miss school instead of vacation, and (4) it would be easier to see inside a dark house in the dark.

2. A shadow of a man appears on the porch with Jem.

3. Jem's pants were snagged on the barbed wire at the Radleys' place, so he left them there. But Jem and Dill told Atticus that Jem had lost them to Dill playing strip poker with matches.

Chapter 7

1. Jem did not tell Scout that when he returned to get his pants they had been mended and folded.

2. Scout finds a boy and girl carved from soap.

3. Scout finds that the knothole has been filled in with cement. Nathan Radley did it, according to him, because the tree was dying.

Chapter 8

1. Scout sees snow.

2. When Jem knows there's not enough snow to build a snowman, he builds the snowman from dirt then covers it with snow.

3. Boo Radley puts the blanket around Scout.

Chapter 9

1. Atticus says this because if he doesn't take this case he will be violating his morals, and if he is immoral he cannot expect his children to obey him.

2. Atticus says this because Tom Robinson is black.

Chapter 10

1. It is a sin to kill a mockingbird because it only makes music for us to enjoy.

2. Calpurnia calls the neighbors so they'll get in their houses and stay off the street.

3. Atticus kills the rabid dog with a single shot.

Chapter 11

1. Student answers will vary (they must give three adjectives to describe Mrs. Dubose), but common answers would be: old, sick, mean, bigoted, brave, vicious, traditional.

2. Lee is using exaggeration.

3. Lee is using a simile.

4. Atticus calls Mrs. Dubose the bravest person he ever knew because she forces herself to give up her morphine addiction even though she is in pain and knows she's dying.

PART 2

Chapter 12

1. They are rudely greeted by one member, but everyone else greets them warmly.

2. The Reverend closes the doors and doesn't let anyone leave until he gets the collection amount he wants.

3. Calpurnia's church doesn't have hymnals because most of the congregation can't read.

Chapter 13

1. Scout defines Fine Folk as those who do the best they could with the sense they had; Aunt Alexandra defines Fine Folk as those whose family have been living on the same land for the longest.

Chapter 14

1. Jem tells Atticus that Dill has run away and come to their house.

2. Dill ran away from home because he feels that his parents get along better without him; he feels that they don't care about him or want him around.

Chapter 15

1. The men who come to the jail want to lynch (kill) Tom Robinson.

2. Atticus is pleased with what Jem did because Jem stood up for Atticus and did what he believed was right.

Chapter 16

1. The people are going into town to watch the trial.

Chapter 17

1. The majority of Sheriff Tate's testimony is about Mayella's injuries.

2. You should never ask a question you don't know the answer to.

3. Atticus wants to show that Ewell is left-handed.

Chapter 18

1. Mayella is afraid of Atticus.

2. It's obvious that Tom did not hit Mayella because she was hit by someone's left hand, and Tom's left hand is crippled.

Chapter 19

1. Student must name three of the following: (1) Mayella says she asked him to chop up the chiffarobe, but Tom says that happened the previous spring; (2) Mayella says she never asked him inside the fence before, Tom says she did; (3) she says she only asked him into the yard, Tom says she asked him into the house; (4) Tom says that Mayella sent the other children away, Mayella won't say where the children were; (5) Mayella says that Tom took advantage of her, Tom says that Mayella grabbed and hugged him; (6) Mayella says that Tom hit her, Tom says he never touched her.

2. The way Mr. Gilmer speaks to Tom makes Dill sick.

Chapter 20

1. The court makes all people equal.

Chapter 21

1. The verdict is guilty.
2. They pay their respects by standing as Atticus walks by.

Chapter 22

1. They show their appreciation by giving him food.
2. Ewell threatens Atticus's life.

Chapter 23

1. Scout finds out that women can't be on juries.
2. Jem says there are four kinds of folks.
3. Jem says background means how long your family's been reading and writing.
4. Scout says there's just one type of folks: folks.

Chapter 24

1. Mrs. Merriweather means Atticus.
2. Mrs. Merriweather is talking about the North and Blacks (slaves).
3. Tom was shot because he tried to escape.

Chapter 25

1. Dill tells Scout the story.
2. It might refer to Tom because it's a sin to kill a mockingbird since they do nothing but give to us, and Tom was killed even though he did nothing but give.
3. Lee uses a metaphor.

Chapter 26

1. Scout doesn't understand how Mrs. Gates can hate Hitler so much for being prejudiced while expressing her own prejudices about the Blacks in Maycomb.

Chapter 27

1. The previous year some of the children snuck into the Barber sisters' house and hid all their furniture in their cellar.

Chapter 28

1. Scout falls asleep and comes out late.

2. Scout is dressed in her ham costume. She's visible because her fat streaks are painted with a shiny paint.

3. Bob Ewell dies.

Chapter 29

1. She thinks it's her fault because she had a feeling that something bad was going to happen yet she did not go with the children to the school.

2. The man is Arthur "Boo" Radley.

Chapter 30

1. Atticus is concerned about the amount of light in the living room because he knows that Arthur isn't used to light and prefers the dark.

2. At first, Atticus thinks Jem killed Bob Ewell.

3. Arthur Radley killed Ewell.

4. Sheriff Tate is going to tell people that Bob Ewell fell on his own knife. He's doing this because he knows if people find out that Arthur did it he will receive a lot of attention that he doesn't want.

5. The title might refer to Arthur because to bring him to the attention of the people of the county would be like killing a mockingbird—he had only done good and telling people what he had done would be a punishment.

Chapter 31

1. Scout does this to preserve Arthur's dignity; this way if anyone sees them it will appear that he is escorting her rather than the other way around.

2. Scout does this to see how things must have looked to Arthur to understand him better.

Literary Lesson: Writing a Literary Analysis

This is an introduction to a complex subject, but it is sufficient to begin the high-school years. As students progress through high-school, they will most likely receive more instruction and feedback on their papers to help hone their skills. The best thing to improve analysis is simply more reading and discussion. I encourage all families to read together and have in-depth discussions about books, short stories, and poems.

Mini-Lesson: Writing a Conclusion

It can be difficult to write a snappy conclusion. For students who have been in the habit of reiterating all the points of the paper in their conclusion, this is a good time to break that habit. As with anything, if they have a teacher who disagrees, it's usually best to bow to the teacher's wishes. More mature writing does not do this, however. As students get more and more papers under their belt, they usually get a stronger natural sense of how to end them. There's no magical formula—it's really just a question of stopping when you're truly finished. Again, as with all things learned in this class, looking at examples in short stories, newspaper articles, magazines, etc., can be instructive.

Writing Exercises

These are equally difficult, but the last two allow the student to get more personal with the paper, which some will prefer. All involve some analysis, so don't feel that your student must do the first one.

Discussion Questions

1. Indirectly, Harper Lee expresses some opinions about schooling in this book. What do you think they are? Do you agree with them? Have you had similar school experiences to any of Scout's?

2. What do you think of Scout's town? How is it similar to your town or neighborhood? How is it different? Do you think the differences have more to do with when this story was set, where the town is, or the size of the town? How would you feel about living in Maycomb?

3. Atticus has to do things that no one else in the town wants to do. Have you ever known anyone who had to do things that no one else wanted to do, but which needed to be done? What was the impact on that person?

What was the impact on that person's loved ones? Why do you think there are people like this in society?

4. Bob Ewell has no redeeming qualities—there is nothing good about this character. Have you ever known, personally, anyone like this? Have you known anyone who seemed all bad?

5. Atticus seems to be all good. There are no obvious faults about his character. Have you ever known, personally, anyone like this? Have you known anyone who seemed all good?

6. Atticus calls Mrs. Dubose brave, and while that is true she is also a mean, unfair bigot. Have you ever known anyone who had both admirable and repulsive characteristics? Who was it? What were they like? Was it difficult to know how you felt about them or know how to interact with them? Is it hard for you to see admirable characteristics in someone who also has many negative characteristics? Would it be helpful in any way for you to do so? If so, how might you get better at this?

7. What do you think of the way Scout, Jem, and Dill treat Boo until the end of the book? Have you ever had a similar mystery in your life? How did you deal with it?

8. A central concern of this book is prejudice. Have you seen prejudice in your life? Have you experienced it? How have you dealt with it?

9. Have you ever felt prejudiced against a group of people? Which group? What was your prejudice against them? Do you still feel any of it? Although the level of prejudice many people in this book express is less common, most of us have small prejudices that we often don't examine. How might it help us to step back and really look at how we view various groups of people?

Answers to Workbook Pages

12.1.A LITERARY ANALYSIS

1. d.

2. This is an example of understatement.

3. This is an example of exaggeration.

4. Twain's first rule applies to plot and author's purpose.

5. Twain's second rule applies to sub-plots.

6. These rules apply to character.

7. These rules apply to dialogue.

8. Twain's sixth rule applies to character and dialogue.

9. These rules apply to language.

10. Twain's fifteenth rule applies to details.

11. This is a poor use of setting.

12. This is a poor use of language.

13. Student must give one of the following: (1) treading in the tracks of the enemy, (2) the broken twig, (3) "the delicate art of the forest," (4) the episode of "the caves," (5) the scuffle between Maqua and others, (6) Hurry Harry's transit from the castle to the ark, (7) Deerslayer's half-hour with his first corpse, and (8) the quarrel between Harry and Deerslayer.

14. Student must give one of the following: (1) "the delicate art of the forest," (2) a ship steered to an undertow to be held against a gale, (3) Bumppo following the track of the cannon-ball, (4) Chingachgook finding someone's tracks under water in a stream, (5) a description of a stream, (6) Indians attacking an ark, (7) the shooting-match in The Pathfinder, Cooper's dialogue

15. This breaks rule number 8.

16. This breaks rule number 9.

17. Twain is using irony.

18. Twain is using metaphor.

19. Twain is using personification.

20. This is an example of irony. (Sarcasm is an acceptable answer, though not as good.)

12.2.P *To Kill a Mockingbird* Crossword Puzzle

12.3.P *To Kill a Mockingbird* Word Search

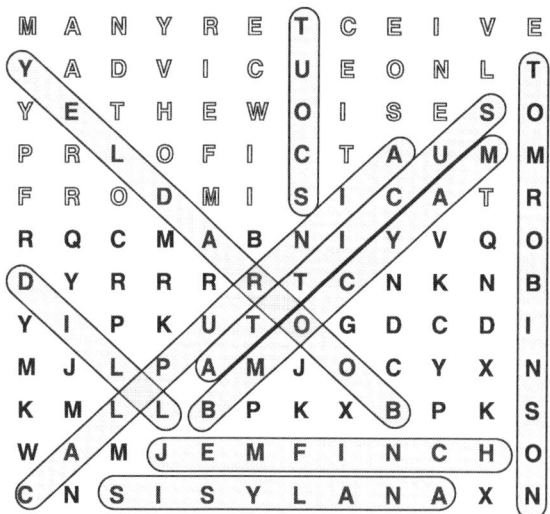

12.4.E THE PERSUASIVE ESSAY

Students should have chosen a narrowly defined topic that is debatable. They should also have given three reasons to support their point of view. The topic sentence should be a statement of position which could be argued (not a fact which can't be debated). The three points should be clearly stated and all be aimed at convincing the reader they have chosen the right point of view. The closing paragraph should review the position they took and three supporting ideas (usually statistics, examples, or specific evidence). New material should **not** be introduced in the closing argument.

Lightning Literature Scope & Sequence

Title & Item Numbers	Literature Covered	Literary Lesson
7th Grade One Year **Junior High: 7th Grade Lightning Lit** #3432 Student Guide #3433 Workbook #3434 Teacher Guide #8081 Pack	1 "Rikki-Tikki-Tavi" by Kipling from *Stories & Poems* 2 *The Adventures of Tom Sawyer* by Mark Twain 3 Selected Poems from *Stories & Poems* 4 *Alice's Adventures in Wonderland* 5 "The Bride Comes to Yellow Sky" by Crane from *Stories & Poems* 6 *The Story of My Life* by Helen Keller 7 Selected Poems from *Stories & Poems* 8 *All Creatures Great and Small* by James Herriot	1 Plot Line 2 Plot Line in a Novel 3 Introduction to Poetry and Rhyme 4 Creativity 5 Dialogue 6 Autobiography 7 Sounds in Poetry 8 Writing about Other People
8th Grade One Year **Junior High 8th Grade Lightning Lit** #3435 Student Guide #3436 Workbook #3437 Teacher Guide #8092 or #8093 Pack	1 "A Crazy Tale" by Chesterton from *Stories & Poems* 2 *Treasure Island* by Robert L. Stevenson 3 *A Day of Pleasure* by Isaac Bashevis Singer 4 "Wakefield" by Hawthorne from *Stories & Poems* 5 *A Christmas Carol* by Charles Dickens 6 *The Hobbit* by J. R. R. Tolkien 7 "Reflections" by Lafcadio Hearn from *Stories & Poems* 8 *My Family and Other Animals* by Gerald Durrell 9 *To Kill a Mockingbird* by Harper Lee 10 Various poets (Whitman, Emerson, Keats, etc.)	1 Author's Purpose 2 Setting 3 Sharing Your Culture 4 Details in Writing 5 Character Development 6 Conflict 7 Symbolism 8 Humor 9 Writing a Literary Analysis 10 Vivid and Figurative Language & Meter
9th to 12th Grade One Semester **American Literature Early to Mid 19th Century Lightning Lit** #3438 Guide #3439 Teacher's Guide #8072 Pack	1 *Autobiography of Benjamin Franklin* 2 "The Angler" by Washington Irving* 3 Poems by William C. Bryant* 4 *Life of Frederick Douglass* 5 "The Tell-Tale Heart" by Edgar A. Poe* 6 *The Scarlet Letter* by Nathaniel Hawthorne 7 *Moby Dick* by Herman Melville 8 Poems by Henry W. Longfellow*	1 Autobiography 2 Sources of Ideas 3 Rhyme and Lines in Poetry 4 Persuasive Writing 5 Tone and Mood 6 Conflict 7 Character Development 8 Meter in Poetry
9th to 12th Grade One Semester **American Literature Mid to Late 19th Century Lightning Lit** #3440 Guide #3441 Teacher's Guide #8073 Pack	1 *Uncle Tom's Cabin* by Harriet B. Stowe 2 *Leaves of Grass* selections by Walt Whitman* 3 "The Outcasts of Poker Flat" by Bret Harte* 4 *The Adv. of Huckleberry Finn* by Mark Twain 5 Poems by Paul Laurence Dunbar* 6 *The Red Badge of Courage* by Stephen Crane 7 Poems by Emily Dickinson* 8 *The Call of the Wild* by Jack London	1 Setting and Theme 2 Sound and Imagery in Poetry 3 Local Color 4 Humor 5 Register 6 Description 7 Figurative Language 8 Point of View
10th to 12th Grade One Semester **British Literature Early to Mid 19th Century Lightning Lit** #3442 Guide #3443 Teacher's Guide #8074 Pack	1 Poems by William Blake* 2 *Pride and Prejudice* by Jane Austen 3 *Ivanhoe* by Sir Walter Scott 4 "Essay on Scott" by Thomas Carlyle* 5 Wordsworth, Coleridge, Byron & Shelley* 6 *Frankenstein* by Mary Shelley 7 *Jane Eyre* by Charlotte Brontë 8 "Rebecca and Rowena" by William Thackeray*	1 Tone 2 Characterization 3 Description 4 Persuasive Writing 5 Imagery & Poetic Language 6 Setting 7 Person 8 Humor
10th to 12th Grade One Semester **British Literature Mid to Late 19th Century Lightning Lit** #3444 Guide #3445 Teacher's Guide #8075 Pack	1 "The Lady of Shalott" by Alfred, Lord Tennyson* 2 *Silas Marner* by George Eliot 3 *Great Expectations* by Charles Dickens 4 Poems by Lewis Carroll* 5 "The Silverado Squatters" by Robert L. Stevenson* 6 *The Importance of Being Earnest* by Oscar Wilde 7 "Adv. of the Speckled Band" by Sir Arthur C. Doyle* 8 *The Complete Stalky & Co* by Rudyard Kipling	1 Rhythm in Poetry 2 Plot 3 Conflict 4 Rhyme in Poetry 5 Local Color 6 Theme 7 Genre: Fiction 8 Sources of Ideas
11th to 12th Grade One Semester **British Medieval Lightning Lit** #3452 Guide #3453 Teacher's Guide #8079 Pack	1 *Beowulf* 2 Anglo-Saxon Riddles* 3 *Piers the Ploughman* 4 "York Mystery Play: The Ascension"* 5 *Sir Gawain and the Green Knight* 6 "The Gest of Robyn Hode"* 7 "The Golden Legend, 'St Thomas Becket'"* 8 *Canterbury Tales* by Geoffrey Chaucer	1 Foreshadowing 2 Metaphor 3 Allegory 4 Theater 5 Tone 6 Ballad 7 Biography 8 Humor

* Included in Guide

✓ Download samples online: www.HewittHS.com

Lightning Literature Scope & Sequence

	Title & Item Numbers	Literature Covered	Literary Lesson
11th to 12th Grade One Semester	**American Christian Authors Lightning Lit** #3458 Guide #3459 Teacher's Guide #8111 Pack	1 Poems by Anne Bradstreet* 2 *Can You Drink the Cup?* by Henri Nouwen 3 "Another Message in a Bottle" by Walker Percy* 4 *A Circle of Quiet* by Madeleine L'Engle 5 Poems by Wendell Berry* 6 *Godric* by Frederick Buechner 7 "The Artificial Nigger" by Flannery O'Connor (online) 8 *No Graven Image* by Elisabeth Elliot	1 Giving a Close Reading 2 Writing a Basic Essay 3 Reading to Respond 4 Writing a Literary Essay 5 Telling the Truth 6 A Biblical Response to Sin in Literature 7 Evaluating Literature Critically 8 Finding a Touchstone
11th to 12th Grade One Semester	**British Christian Authors Lightning Lit** #3456 Guide #3457 Teacher's Guide #8080 Pack	1 *The Four Loves* by C. S. Lewis 2 *Phantastes* selection by George MacDonald* 3 Poems by Gerard Manley Hopkins* 4 *Why Does God Allow War?* by D. MartynLloyd-Jones 5 "The Gold Cord" by Amy Carmichael* 6 *Orthodoxy* by G. K. Chesterton 7 Poems by T. S. Eliot 8 *Gaudy Night* by Dorothy Sayers	1 Writing a Five Paragraph Essay 2 Symbolism 3 Word Choice, Imagery, Syntax in Poetry 4 Writing Clearly 5 Writing for a Reason 6 Writing to Persuade 7 Writing Literary Analysis 8 Choosing Subject Matter
11th to 12th Grade One Semester	**Shakespeare Tragedies and Sonnets Lightning Lit** #3446 Guide #3447 Teacher's Guide #8076 Pack	1 *Julius Caesar* 2 Sonnets 5 & 6* 3 *Hamlet* 4 Sonnets 73 & 97* 5 *Macbeth* 6 Sonnets 29 & 30* 7 *King Lear* 8 Sonnets 18 & 65*	Shakespearean Lightning Lit Guides include plot summaries, and cover literary analysis of each work by looking at setting, theme, perspective, characters, symbolism, imagery, and stage directions.
11th to 12th Grade One Semester	**Shakespeare Comedies and Sonnets Lightning Lit** #3448 Guide #3449 Teacher's Guide #8077 Pack	1 *Twelfth Night* 2 Sonnets 27 & 28* 3 *As You Like It* 4 Sonnets 130 & 136* 5 *A Midsummer Night's Dream* 6 Sonnet 93 & 138* 7 *The Merchant of Venice* 8 Sonnets 116 & 129*	Shakespearean Lightning Lit Guides include plot summaries, and cover literary analysis of each work by looking at setting, theme, perspective, characters, symbolism, imagery, and stage directions.
11th to 12th Grade One Semester	**World Literature 1 Africa and Asia** #3460 Guide #3461 Teacher's Guide #8094 Pack	1 *Things Fall Apart* by Chinua Achebe 2 African Poetry in *This Same Sky* by Naomi Shihab Nye 3 *An Artist of the Floating World* by Kazuo Ishiguro 4 Poetry of the Far East in *This Same Sky* 5 *Fountain and Tomb* by Naguib Mahfoauz 6 Middle Eastern Poetry in *This Same Sky* 7 Autobiography (chosen from list) 8 Poetry as Life Story in *This Same Sky*	1 Historical Fiction 2 Sounds of Poetry 3 Point of View 4 Themes of Poetry 5 Symbolism in Literature 6 Imagery in Poetry 7 Autobiography 8 Tone
11th to 12th Grade One Semester	**World Literature 2 Latin America, India, Japan, and China** #3462 Guide #3463 Teacher's Guide #8095 Pack	1 *Malgudi Days* by H. K. Narayan 2 Short Stories of India from *Other Voices, Other Vistas* 3 *My Invented Country* by Isabel Allende 4 Short Stories of Latin America/Japan (*Other Voices, Other Vistas*) 5 *A Thousand Pieces of Gold* by Adeline Yen Mah 6 Short Stories of China (*Other Voices, Other Vistas*) 7 *In the Name of Identity* by Amin Maalouf 8 Short Stories of Africa (*Other Voices, Other Vistas*)	1 Developing Characters 2 Style and Irony 3 Descriptive Writing 4 Setting 5 Writing about History—People and Events 6 Political Fiction and Satire 7 Persuasive Writing 8 Conflict and Plot
9th to 12th Grade One Semester	**Speech Lightning Lit** #3450 Guide #3451 Teacher's Guide #8091 Pack	*Lend Me Your Ears* by William Safire	1 *Opening* 2 *Content* 3 *Research and Factual Argument* 4 *Organization* 5 *Audience* 6 *Words and Sentences* 7 *Rhetorical Style* 8 *Conclusion*

* Included in Guide

ISBN 978-1-57896-237-2

9 781578 962372